Making Moral Decisions

A Christian Approach to Personal and Social Ethics

PAUL JERSILD

Fortress Press Minneapolis

To my parents, in gratitude

Hans Christian Jersild (1896–1968)
Carrie Sinamark Jersild

MAKING MORAL DECISIONS
A Christian Approach to Personal and Social Ethics

Scripture quotations unless otherwise noted are from the Revised Standard Version of the Bible, copyright © 1946, 1952, and 1971 by the Division of Christian Education of the National Council of Churches.

Cover design: Hilber Nelson

Library of Congress Cataloging-in-Publication Data
Jersild, Paul T., 1931–
    Making moral decisions : a Christian approach to personal and
social ethics / Paul Jersild.
        p.   cm.
    Includes bibliographical references and index.
    ISBN 0-8006-2471-8 (alk. paper)
    1. Christian ethics—Lutheran authors.   2. Social ethics.
3. Decision-making (Ethics)   I. Title.
BJ1251.J375   1990
241'.0441—dc20   90-44766
                                                                                              CIP

The paper used in this publication meets the minimum requirements of American National Standard for Information Sciences—Permanence of Paper for Printed Library Materials, ANSI Z329.48–1984.   ∞ ™

Manufactured in the U.S.A.   AF 1-2471

CONTENTS

3

PREFACE

A subject as complex and demanding as moral decision making continually invites the insights of those who have thought carefully about it. Such insights reveal not only the individual life experience of the author but also the religious and cultural traditions that have formed that life experience and that provide both substance and nuance to what each has to say.[1] I write both as an individual and also as a member of a Christian community shaped and inspired by the Reformation tradition and particularly by the specific heritage of the Lutheran church. At the same time, my point of view assumes that every tradition within the household of faith not only has moral insight to offer but also stands in need of instruction and balance from the rest of the household.

A particular concern of this book is to unite individual moral decision making with the moral responsibility of the Christian community. The assumption is that we cannot treat the moral decision making of individual Christians apart from the church in which they find community. This is true not only in the sense that each of us is shaped by the community of faith that has nurtured us but also because our moral responsibility as Christians embraces our life together. I am concerned that Christians see moral decision making in terms of "we" as well as "I," that we recognize moral obligation automatically as both an individual and corporate responsibility. What am I to do? needs the balance and completion of, What are we to do? as a Christian community in this world.

Thus the reader will note that the final two chapters address the response of the church to the moral challenges of our time, broadening our individual responsibility to that of the church as a moral community. A particular need of our time, often noted in recent literature, is greater consciousness of our interdependence as a society and as a world community. The church must take that issue with great seriousness, recognizing that its very nature as a worldwide community that transcends national and ideological boundaries lays a heavy responsibility on its shoulders. It has a message and a vision inspired by its faith that can both challenge and renew this world, but not until Christians as individuals and as the church take their faith and their moral commitments seriously.

Particularly in this period of moral confusion in Western society and even within the church itself, the community of faith needs to think critically about moral decision making. We need to see that the moral quality of our individual lives bears directly on the moral quality of our life together, and vice versa. We face a growing imperative as individuals and as a society to forge a moral community marked by justice and concern for all of God's people and the whole of creation. An ethic of this kind, which is sensitive to the common good, will challenge us to find our individual fulfillment in lives that contribute to the quality of our life together. This is the nature of Christian ethics itself, in which individuals find themselves precisely by losing themselves on behalf of others. This old and powerful message is as profound and as needed today as ever.

This book is directed primarily toward the educated layperson who is serious about reflecting on the nature of the Christian life. It is informed by scholarly works, but is intended to be readable and engaging for those whose backgrounds do not include the academic study of ethics. References to other works are therefore kept to a minimum. I must acknowledge, however, the influence of numerous writers in the field of Christian ethics who through their books and articles have been the teachers of many of us who labor in the classroom—including in my own case such giants as Reinhold and H. Richard Niebuhr, Helmut Thielicke, Paul Ramsey, and James Gustafson.

I am indebted to several people for their reading of this manuscript, either in whole or in part, and contributing helpful critique. In particular, I want to mention two colleagues at the Lutheran Southern Seminary, Michael Root and Carl Ficken. The weaknesses that remain can be attributed to no one but myself. I also want to thank my wife, Marilyn, who has often been a model as well as a helpful conversation partner on matters relating to the contents of this book. And finally, a note of thanks to the seminary and to student Virginia Barnes for their assistance in bringing the manuscript to completion.

LUTHERAN THEOLOGICAL SOUTHERN SEMINARY
COLUMBIA, SOUTH CAROLINA

1 ⟩ BEING A CHRISTIAN IN TODAY'S WORLD

Morality is a controversial subject for every generation. It is a rare commentator on contemporary morality who is not concerned by the unraveling of moral standards and the prevalence of moral confusion. Handwringing and prophecies of doom are common enough in every age to make some people quite fearful—and others quite skeptical—that things could really be so bad. Indeed, we are not well served by pessimists who want to see the worst in every changing moral scene. Nonetheless, a discriminating assessment of current morality reveals much that is discouraging and even threatening to the welfare of our society.

Because we live in a social environment that conditions and shapes our moral responses, we should not ignore changes taking place in our world. From the beginning, Christians seeking to live a faithful life have had to confront the larger environment with its many challenges and perils. Whether the church is a persecuted sect or part of a respected establishment, Christians never encounter a world in which they can live in complete harmony. The task of Christians in every age and place is to understand their social environment in order to perceive more clearly the moral challenges they face and the significance of those challenges for Christian life. Understanding the dynamics affecting the morality of our times enables us to be forearmed as we seek to determine the character of responsible Christian living.

Moral Confusion in Our Society

During the last several decades our society has become increasingly pluralistic; we have become more diverse and no longer
share in a common religious and moral tradition. Many Christian
writers have exhorted us not to be fearful in this situation but
to welcome the openness, freedom, and genuine dialogue made
possible in a society that is no longer dominated by a monolithic
tradition. Others, however, find it difficult to share this enthu-
siasm. An opposing view was expressed by the television evangelist and presidential candidate, Pat Robertson, in a 1987
interview: "Pluralism is the name given to the transition period
from one orthodoxy to another. . . . Every other great nation
has unified around some ethical standard. Lack of unity is a sign
of ultimate destruction."[1]

Robertson has what we call a triumphalist vision of Christianity: a religion on the march, molding the nation into an
instrument of God that will vanquish the enemy. That vision
finds it difficult—if not impossible—to accept the heterogeneity
of our citizens and the waning influence of the Christian tradition
(in spite of much lip service given to it) on public life. One may
not use the apocalyptic language of "ultimate destruction," but
clearly, because religion serves as the foundation for a society's
moral beliefs, the weakening of the religious tradition will bring
with it a certain amount of moral confusion. Elton Trueblood
used more radical language some forty years ago to describe the
West as a "cut-flower" civilization in which the religious roots
of our culture were being severed; consequently, the common
moral life nurtured by that tradition could not long survive.[2]

Many writers have noted the moral bewilderment we are
now experiencing. Historians and philosophers are particularly
alert to these kinds of developments. Historian Barbara Tuchman
notes that our times have been marked by "real deterioration in
public morality." She describes "an age of disruption," one in
which we have lost our belief in traditional understandings of
good and bad. Says Tuchman, "I think [this loss of belief] has
left many people feeling uneasy, because . . . they don't know
how to behave, they don't know what's right and what's wrong.[3]

The confusion runs deep. It is not just a matter of people
beginning to question their previous views on moral issues such

as abortion or premarital sex. People are questioning the existence of an objective order of moral truth. The idea that morality reflects no more than the subjective tastes or personal likes and dislikes of the individual is a possibility long discussed by philosophers, but we now find this notion prevalent in popular culture. If we can no longer refer to one commonly acknowledged moral tradition, then to many it appears that no moral reality governs right and wrong apart from the opinion of the individual or the individual's group. Or, if an objective moral reality exists, it no longer appears to be self-evident; no one speaks with authority.

This loss of confidence in moral judgments is reflected in the uneasiness many people feel about the use of language associated with moral judgments. Even people of strong moral conviction find themselves uneasy about using such words as *right* and *wrong* because the slightest hint of moral judgment is commonly regarded as evidence of moralism or legalism. It is as though any expression of moral judgment is an unworthy assault on another person's freedom.

As a consequence, the tendency today is to substitute other language for words that sound too moral. Rather than saying a particular action is the *right* thing to do, we call it a sensible, helpful, or appropriate thing to do. Instead of risking the judgment that a particular action is *wrong*, we might venture the judgment that it is inappropriate, unfortunate, or (if we feel particularly strong about it) even stupid or foolish. We use the overtly moral terms only at the risk of appearing naive and causing embarrassment, for they are out of step with the "enlightened" attitudes of society.

As a result of our unwillingness to exercise moral judgment, we are also experiencing an unwillingness to fix blame. Since the 1960s, we have been sensitized to the impact of society on the individual; a poverty-stricken environment will push many young people into antisocial activities, and society as a whole shares a responsibility for those whose blighted lives result in destructive behavior. Nonetheless, each person faces a moral imperative that challenges him or her to live responsibly. A poor environment does not excuse the practice of evil. As Tuchman notes, we forget the neighbors of the criminal who were equally poor and equally disadvantaged but did *not* resort to criminal activities. At the same time, fixing blame is both an individual and corporate matter; the larger society cannot avoid blame for its ghettos of poverty and hopelessness.

The "deterioration in public morality" noted by Tuchman has been richly documented by many commentators. Perhaps most prominent in these reviews is the recognition of a society "on the take." One author sees the guiding principle of our society in the expectation that "one should maximize one's share of society's riches as quickly as possible. The end justifies whatever means are necessary to attain that goal."[4] The consumer society is seen as the villain in accentuating the "get-rich-quick" syndrome, with all of its banality and excesses. In the colorful words of Norman Lear, "America has become a game show. Winning is all that matters. Cash prizes. Get rich quick. We are captives of a culture that celebrates instant gratification and individual success no matter the larger costs."[5]

The suggestion that our culture encourages individuals to look out for themselves at the expense of the community is a major thesis of a recent work on the American character entitled *Habits of the Heart.*[6] The authors argue that Americans have exalted individual autonomy and freedom to the point of a crisis in values. The individual has become the source and judge of what is good and evil, resulting in the loss of a common morality to which society is accountable. Values are dependent upon one's personal preferences, and since each person is unique, it is inappropriate for anyone to make moral judgment of another. The result is moral confusion.

> What is good is what one finds rewarding. If one's preferences change, so does the nature of the good. Even the deepest ethical virtues are justified as matters of personal preference. Indeed, the ultimate ethical rule is simply that individuals should be able to pursue whatever they find rewarding, constrained only by the requirement that they not interfere with the "value systems" of others.[7]

It is difficult to find two concepts more appealing and persuasive to the American mind than individualism and freedom.

Together they seem to capture the essence of our character as a people, yet if they are understood in certain ways they become concepts that can also threaten our common life. Freedom has come to mean little more than being left alone; it is our claim to our own bit of space in which we can exercise personal moral autonomy. We want to define freedom in egocentric terms: a freedom from what appears to be the arbitrary authority of others—family, superiors at work, the church, the government. We fail to recognize that freedom is a state of opportunity that enables us to commit ourselves to those values and goals that deserve our allegiance. Our problem as a people is that we claim personal freedom as a right but we don't know what to do with it. It is simply a freedom *from* without being a freedom *for*.

This view of freedom creates an atmosphere of "each one for oneself," as in the story of two men backpacking in the northern woods. As they made a turn in the trail, they suddenly encountered a cougar and stopped dead in their tracks. One man slowly began to slip out of his backpack, drawing an incredulous eye from his friend. "Do you really think you can outrun him?" his friend asked. "That's not the point," came the reply. "All I've got to do is outrun you." This story reveals more about our society than we care to admit!

The authors of *Habits of the Heart* also relate the moral confusion in our society to the "therapeutic consciousness," or the impact of therapy as a cultural phenomenon. They see this consciousness, which has become dominant in the middle class over the last few decades, as a way of thinking that centers upon the need to "find" oneself. To reach this goal we must get in touch with our feelings and affirm them. Our psychic and emotional needs are accentuated, with the assumption that fulfilling them is synonymous with self-fulfillment. The individual has become autonomous, the self a source of moral direction for whom "being good" is "feeling good."[8]

For the therapeutic self, questions of right and wrong become questions of finding what I need to bring self-realization or personal happiness. Right and wrong are translated into what works for me or what does not work for me, with little or no sensibility to the dangers of egoism inherent to this self-understanding.

What is essential is that I know my needs in order to relate to others in ways that will satisfy those needs. One works with a "contractual model" in relating to others, willing to compromise as necessary but holding to the course that satisfies one's personal needs. The impact of this model upon long-term human relationships—as in marriage—is obviously problematic. It applies a "giving-in-order-to-get" attitude governed by one's own self-interests, an attitude that may be appropriate in certain relationships but is inadequate and even destructive when it begins to dominate those intimate and enduring personal commitments that lend stability and identity to one's life.[9]

The crisis we face is the loss of common ground for the moral judgments we make. Therefore, the individual reigns supreme when it comes to ethics or moral reasoning. The tradition that has informed and shaped our vision of the good life no longer holds the authority it once did and thus no longer provides convincing support and direction for the conduct of our lives. The crisis is accentuated by the dramatic impact of science and technology, changing our world and the ways in which we relate to each other. The pace of social change, together with the weakening of our moral tradition, heightens our apprehensions and uncertainty. Christians share in this unsettling kind of environment, but they also have their community of faith to provide support in meeting these challenges. While one might expect this community to provide a clear and coherent moral stance, informing and supporting the individual Christian, this is not necessarily the case.

Is There a Christian Morality?

If there are particular challenges for Christians in today's society, there is also much that is confusing within the Christian community itself. For one thing, we apparently have no unified response to the challenges that society presents to the church. The divisions within society are often mirrored within the church, and disagreements over moral issues can be as intense, if not more so, within the church as outside it. An incident involving two couples, both of them seriously committed Christians, illustrates the problem.

John and Blanche are active members of First Baptist Church. In addition to being regular worshipers, they have particularly appreciated the adult class conducted each Sunday by their pastor. Pastor Bledsoe decided to devote a whole year to a series of courses addressing controversial social issues, and attendance dramatically increased as word got around that class discussion was candid and generally well informed. Members of the class volunteered to serve as resource people on those topics that were of particular interest to them, and many of them read extensively in preparation for the class. Especially helpful was the attempt on the part of everyone to relate Christian convictions to the subject being discussed. John and Blanche had always been concerned about the church's witness in regard to public policy issues and were themselves important resources in the discussion of a number of topics. They were highly critical of their nation's defense policy, in which the Pentagon's budget had increased at a much higher rate than in previous years. They thought of nuclear war as obscene and wanted much more rigor and imagination in the pursuit of arms reduction than was presently the case.

They also had strong feelings about capital punishment. They were adamantly opposed to it—Blanche on grounds of principle and John more on pragmatic grounds. Blanche's views were basically pacifist: she took seriously the radical summons to nonviolence that she perceived in the teachings of Jesus. Understanding and rehabilitation, not vindictive punishment, were the answer. John was not convinced that the death penalty really worked in deterring people from committing capital crimes; otherwise he'd be for it.

At one of the semiannual meetings of the Midlands Ecumenical Council, an organization in the metropolitan area that included some seventy churches representing eleven different denominations, John and Blanche met Fred and Tina, who were members of Asbury Methodist Church. John and Fred were both employed by companies manufacturing personal computers, and they quickly found themselves at home "talking shop." The women discovered some common interests from their professional and personal lives and were soon enjoying each other's company.

The couples decided to continue their conversation at a nearby restaurant. Fred and Tina were dedicated members of Asbury Methodist and headed the Evangelism and Outreach Committee. They had attended the ecumenical meeting that evening because of the speaker, a popular evangelist known for his eloquence as a preacher.

Soon after sitting down at the restaurant, John expressed disappointment with the message because it had not brought the listeners into touch with the realities they faced in the world.

"All he talked about was my personal relation to Jesus," complained John. "The trouble with the church today is that it never gets off that subject. It becomes an escape from the real world, a religious trip that invites us to turn our backs on where the action is, where tough decisions have to be made. That's where our convictions are really put to the test."

Fred and Tina were quick to express their disagreement with John. "He really spoke to me," said Tina. "He was preaching the gospel that puts us all in a one-to-one relation with Jesus. This is the most important thing; nothing else really matters."

Fred took up Tina's argument. "We have to be careful we don't reduce the gospel to morality, which usually means *my* morality. An ecumenical event like tonight's meeting has to center on the gospel message; bringing in social issues would only be divisive."

John was getting uncomfortable and decided to change the subject. He motioned to the bar adjoining the restaurant and asked if he could get everyone a beer. Fred and Tina looked at each other and shook their heads. "We get along well without alcohol," remarked Fred. Blanche suggested coffee and the others agreed.

Conversation was a bit restrained as the couples sensed they were on different wavelengths. Blanche began to talk about the adult class at First Baptist and the excitement people were sharing. She mentioned several topics the class had discussed, and Fred began to shake his head.

"I've never understood," he observed, "how one could be a pacifist. The state *must* defend its citizens. The same goes for capital punishment. The state must reserve the right to destroy those who insist on destroying others. People who don't see that are living in some other world than the real one."

There was a momentary silence as John and Blanche considered whether to argue the point. Tina attempted to ease the embarrassment by noting that Christians often do find themselves on opposite sides of social issues. "The most important thing," she said, "is whether Christians are really willing to follow Christ in the way they live their individual lives. Is a person related to Jesus Christ *personally* in worship and prayer? Is a person really willing to tithe? Is a person willing to live a simple or even austere life and then support others who are in greater need? Is a person willing to give a year or more to work on the mission field? These are the critical issues of Christian commitment, not where one stands on complex social issues."

As they drove home that night, John and Blanche tried to sort out the implications of what had been said.

"It seems to me," said John, "that Christians disagree as much on matters of personal life-style and individual Christian commitment as they do on the big social issues of the day. Fred and Tina make me uncomfortable—just a bit too serious and strait-laced for me."

"It makes you wonder," mused Blanche, "if there is any such thing as a Christian way of life or Christian morality, to say nothing of a Christian approach to social issues. Maybe we can't expect Baptists and Methodists to agree on these matters, but there's plenty of disagreement within each church, too. I guess I'm more confused than anything else."

Many of us have shared Blanche's bewilderment. We might phrase the problem in terms of a question: What does it mean to be a Christian? In terms of confessing our faith, it appears relatively simple. The early Christian confession, "Jesus is Lord," served to identify the Christian community. Christ is at the center of life, the one sovereign Lord over all powers on earth, our final source of confidence and hope. This affirmation can be analyzed ad infinitum and theologians can disagree on the finer points, but Christians from around the world can still celebrate their fundamental unity as expressed in the ecumenical creeds or other common confessions.

Defining a moral life to which all Christians could commit themselves does not appear so simple. There is no straight line from theological confession to moral practice. What does the lordship of Jesus Christ mean for each of us in making moral decisions? How is this confession, this allegiance, to be translated into our daily lives in terms of our response to personal and social issues that surround each of us?

If one seeks an answer to these questions by observing what Christians in fact do with their lives, it becomes evident that there are many contradictory answers to these questions. The four persons in the incident just described are clearly serious about their Christian commitment, but this seriousness does not always express itself in the same ways. They reveal differences in their views of worship, the Christian's relation to Jesus Christ, the shape of personal living as a follower of Christ, and the stance taken concerning any number of social issues.

Why Do Christians Disagree on Moral Issues?

We can define the Christian moral life as the commitment of believers to live a responsible life in light of their faith in the biblical story that culminates in Jesus Christ. Christian faith by its very nature issues from a life of obedience or response to the gospel of Jesus Christ. Of course, this general statement leaves much to be said concerning the Christian's resources for moral decision making and what should be understood by a "responsible life" (subjects that are addressed in subsequent chapters). As illustrated by the case study, Christian commitment in itself does not automatically bring unanimity among Christians in their moral judgments, whether one is addressing public issues or matters of personal morality. The more serious one becomes in studying the nature of Christian life, the more one recognizes that there is no "quick fix" to moral issues, no obvious solution guaranteed to Christians or easily identified by everyone as the "Christian" answer.

One reason for this is that moral issues can be quite complicated. A moral topic becomes an "issue" because equally well-informed and discerning individuals find themselves in disagreement about it. This will happen *among* Christians as much as *between* Christians and non-Christians. Equally discerning and committed Christians can disagree over issues such as abortion or capital punishment because these issues involve a host of conflicting values that are not easily resolved. As much as we would like our moral decisions to be clear-cut and obvious, sufficient ambiguity often leaves us uncertain about what we should do.

Furthermore, the issue may be difficult to relate to the Christian tradition. We would like to have a decisive word from Scripture to resolve the issue, but the issue may be a moral dilemma that the biblical writers could never have imagined, much less

addressed. Many situations can be found in bioethics, for example, where medical technology has altered the circumstances
surrounding both birth and death, resulting in dramatically new
and difficult decisions involving the value of life under varying
conditions.

Also, some obvious environmental factors lead us in different
directions in our approach to moral issues. We are more aware
today than ever that no one is raised in a strictly neutral environment as far as the development of one's moral outlook is
concerned. This occurs even among Christians living in the same
cultural setting, particularly when they are raised under the influence of distinctive traditions that place them at odds with the
majority of Christians.

For example, both the Mennonite Church and the Church
of the Brethren espouse pacifism. This radical commitment to
nonviolence is the distinguishing mark of these churches, and
many who have received from them their Christian training have
also absorbed the spirit of pacifism. It is a stance that for them
identifies Christian commitment, even if it is a stance not shared
by most Christians.

One area of personal living on which John and Blanche and
Fred and Tina were at odds, and one that has agitated many
Christians in our society, is the consumption of alcoholic beverages. Christians have long been found on both sides of this
issue. Though many would discount the subject as not worth
serious moral discussion, others who have experienced the blight
of alcoholism believe it demands careful evaluation on the part
of the Christian community.

In his "general rules," John Wesley, the founder of Methodism, forbade the drinking of "spiritous liquors." This kind of
behavior did not fit with the seriousness of the Christian pil-
grimage. Methodism provided the religious roots for the tem-
perance movement that finally led to the passing of the
Eighteenth Amendment in 1919, prohibiting "the manufacture,
sale, or transportation of intoxicating liquors."

Despite the public support given this moral judgment at the
time (the amendment was repealed within fifteen years), many
Christians were not in favor of it. Beer-drinking Lutherans, whose

roots in the Old World included appreciation of fine draft beer, saw no contradiction with their Christian life in having beer with a meal. Many Catholics and Episcopalians were also accustomed to social drinking, finding no moral or religious problem in the use of alcohol when it was handled with moderation. Most Christians today would likely place the issue in the realm of Christian freedom, arguing that one should not attempt to establish a universal law regarding the consumption of alcohol. Nonetheless, the attitudes of Christians on this subject will usually reflect the particular history and experience of their denomination.

We could of course multiply these cases, but they illustrate the point. Whether it is a public issue of considerable importance or an issue of personal morality, Christians are likely to be found on opposing sides. Sometimes this may result from the distinctive experience and teaching of one's particular church. But factors apart from the church or the Christian tradition will also influence one's moral attitudes.

One's economic class, for example, is a powerful factor in shaping one's moral judgments as they relate to the economic and social order. If we are solid middle-class citizens, we are usually in no position to understand the concerns of the poor as they relate to economic policies. The economic life of our society is shaped by the interaction of competing interests, and we naturally identify with the interests of our own class. This does not have to be a consciously selfish choice, but one that naturally makes sense to us. We see things from where we are standing.

Another example concerns one's education. Professional people will generally find it difficult to appreciate the concerns and needs of the less-educated working class. Education and economic class are joint contributors in shaping the political and social priorities one has, which in turn has an impact on the way one perceives moral issues that underlie public policy decisions. When educated middle-class people look at issues of public welfare, for example, questions of costs and who's going to pay them loom large. Because the benefits of welfare are not seen as benefits to the middle class, all they are prone to see is the bite it will take out of their own pocketbook. The morality of the issue is dominated by their perception that people are inherently greedy; if they can live off welfare, they will.

On the other hand, Christians and non-Christians alike who are struggling to keep their heads above water economically are tempted to share certain stereotyped judgments about the rich and the powerful. They may easily assume a cynical attitude toward "the establishment," which actually results in a warped view of reality. Resentment over our own lack of success in economic or occupational achievement can lead us to blame others for creating the society that has failed to give us a break. Thus, the deviousness of the human heart leads both the "haves" and the "have-nots" to project the worst of human motivations upon each other.

Whether it be the uniqueness of one's own Christian moral tradition, the complicated and ambiguous nature of moral issues in the personal and public policy realms, or the impact of one's own economic or social groups, Christians will find themselves in disagreement. No matter how seriously John and Blanche and Fred and Tina had attempted to work out the implications of their common faith for the moral issues they were discussing that night, they would probably not have come to complete agreement. Most of the reasons for this are at least understandable, though they are not always justifiable.

This picture of moral disagreement both inside and outside of the Christian community poses a confused and perhaps even a depressing spectacle for many Christians. We are being challenged to reflect long and hard about the moral grounds on which we act, and about the ways in which we arrive at moral decisions. Our understandable desire for clear and convincing answers to personal and social dilemmas may not be satisfied, which is a reality we simply must live with. Whatever the ambiguities, we are obligated as Christians to take our discipleship seriously as individuals and as a community of faith, seeking to live a life worthy of the gospel of Jesus Christ. To live that kind of life is demanding in any age, whatever the cultural or social circumstances. It is our particular challenge—and privilege—to be faithful in this time and place.

The following chapters will seek to explore the resources for Christians in making moral decisions and will analyze the elements involved in our decision making. Incidents from every-day life will dramatize several areas in which we can face some difficult moral dilemmas. The final two chapters will widen our focus from the Christian individual to the Christian community and the challenge it faces in addressing the social issues of our day. Here decision making takes on a corporate character as the community of faith seeks to live in faithfulness to its witness and to its Lord, Jesus Christ.

THE BIBLE AS AUTHORITY FOR MORAL LIFE

2

Christianity is one of the world religions that has relied heavily on a sacred scripture. As the foundation document of Christian faith, the Bible bears an authority for the faith and life of the church that no other document can claim. At the same time, Christians will disagree over the nature and extent of biblical authority. This is certainly true in regard to the Bible's role and authority for the moral life. Recognizing that the biblical materials reflect in many ways the moral standards and values of ancient Israel and of the early Christian community, contemporary Christians are compelled to choose some principle of interpretation to determine a consistent and appropriate understanding of the Bible's moral authority for today. What should Christians expect from the Bible in equipping them for responsible moral decision making?

The Use of Scripture in Making Decisions

One can cite at least five different approaches to the use of Scripture as a moral resource.[1]

1. *The Bible provides a moral code or set of commandments.* Some have emphasized those parts of Scripture that convey moral imperatives or exhortations, finding in this material the moral basis for Christian living. This view will assume that a commandment can be found in the Scriptures for every situation encountered by the Christian. The challenge is to find the proper

imperative and match it with the occasion or the temptation. The Ten Commandments (Exodus 20) would be the basic moral resource, but other imperatives can be found that supplement and make more concrete the moral requirements expressed in the Decalogue. The Bible gives us a moral code through its many commandments, and with proper direction we can use it as a reliable handbook for the moral life. This view typically assumes that there is a unity to the moral imperatives found in the Scriptures, binding together both the Old and the New Testament.

2. *The Bible provides moral direction through the example of people of faith.* Rather than treating the Scriptures as a self-sufficient moral handbook with specific directives, we can find moral nurture and inspiration by considering the lives of men and women of faith who are portrayed in the pages of Scripture. The struggles and example of such figures as Moses, King David, Deborah, Ruth, the Apostle Paul, and of course Jesus himself, help us to perceive the secret of moral responsibility and faithful living. The moral significance of the biblical message is found primarily in the embodiment of values in the lives of its characters and in the stories we find there. From the narratives of Scripture, the writers will sometimes reflect on the moral dimensions of life, but more often the reader is left to think about the moral principles to be gleaned from the stories.

3. *The Bible's moral impact flows from God's involvement in history as Creator, Redeemer, and Sanctifier.* This view believes it is more fruitful to focus on the God revealed in the Bible and the implications this revelation of God has for our common life than to attempt to find either specific directives or particular principles embedded in the narrative material of Scripture. For example, the God of Scripture is the Creator who calls us to account; we are thus stewards of God's creation, which means that Christians ought to be concerned about ecology. Caring for the world of nature is both a theological and moral imperative. This approach is more conceptual, basing moral imperatives in theological truths supported by biblical material rather than directly from biblical passages themselves.

4. *The Bible reveals God's plan of salvation, while our moral response depends on our particular church heritage.* The Bible brings

the believer into the presence of God and creates a community of believers who are committed to Jesus Christ. As far as the individual's discipleship and moral life are concerned, the traditions of that faithful community create the shape and pattern of response. Those traditions will reflect the theological heritage, the way in which Scripture is understood, and the historical development of that community. Responsible interpretation of Scripture can provide theoretical foundation for the moral life, but the tradition of the individual's faith community or church will give the concrete moral direction for faithful living.

5. *The Bible does not in fact give us a unified, coherent basis for moral life.* This view makes a more radical judgment than number 4 above, stressing the uselessness of any attempt to find a broad and coherent moral theme in Scripture that could provide a basis for moral direction. It emphasizes the selectivity of every attempt to find a basis for the moral life in Scripture, arguing that its variety of moral expression defies any notion of a revealed morality. Consequently, in order to avoid misuse of the Bible or false expectations, it is best to make clear that it does not serve this purpose. One will simply use it to reinforce one's preconceived notion of what the Scriptures say about the moral life.[2]

These understandings of Scripture and the moral life should not be regarded as exclusive alternatives, as though one were absolutely correct and all the others wrong. Even the fifth viewpoint, which is too extreme to be an adequate answer, contains an element of truth that should not be overlooked. One might agree that the Bible as a whole does not present a unified, coherent moral theory, and yet one might find in the New Testament a continuity in the moral teachings of Jesus and of Paul that captures the essential moral contribution of the Bible for the Christian community. One may agree that we are not to search for moral imperatives in Scripture as the way to confirm its moral relevance for today, and yet at the same time one may well acknowledge imperatives, either explicit or implicit in the Bible, that we must hear today.

It is fair to say that the Bible is not primarily a book on morality or a book devoted to the moral life. At the same time, as a book that serves a people of faith, it contains much material of great moral substance. The life of faith is a life called to moral responsibility; otherwise, one's faith becomes the victim of sentimentality or religious aestheticism. A moral seriousness runs throughout Scripture, a seriousness that is reflected in the community of faith as it earnestly seeks in every generation to be doing the will of the Lord. Though these sacred writings cannot be expected to speak directly to us in the face of every moral issue, much has been and will continue to be morally edifying and helpful for Christians of every age.

Nonetheless, many of the imperatives and moral attitudes in the Bible do not constitute the final word for us today. We are far removed from that Old Testament morality in which children are destroyed for making fun of a prophet (2 Kings 2:23-24) or a family is killed because of one man's theft (Joshua 7). Laws in the Old Testament governing the relations of men and women have little to say to us because the status of women in Israel was quite different from the status of women today. Or the question of capital punishment is addressed in the Old Testament from such a different social and cultural perspective that it fails to fully engage the issues with which we are grappling today. A common punishment in ancient Israel for anything from adultery to idol worship was the death penalty; to seek counsel from the Old Testament codes concerning this subject and many others is to deny the rest of our history as a community of faith.

The subject of war is another example we might cite. The Old Testament reveals a development in its own thinking on this topic. In early Israelite history, God speaks as a "man of war" who leads the people into battle (Exod. 15:3). This God commands the people to utterly wipe out civilian populations, including the women and children, as an act of divine vengeance (Numbers 31). As time goes on, a quite different perspective emerges with the prophets, and Israel is exhorted not to take up the sword but to trust in the Lord God who will save the people from destruction. This exhortation to leave the expression of wrath to God and to pray for one's enemies reaches its highest expression in the teachings of Jesus (Matthew 5). Clearly, to expect a word from Scripture concerning warfare requires considerable interpretation and a method for determining which material in Scripture should be decisive.

We conclude that to affirm the Scriptures as authoritative for moral issues and moral behavior is going to reveal some kind of selective principle. This is true in any kind of interpretation of the biblical message. The important thing is that our principle of interpretation embody the essential message of Scripture so that our understanding of it is not skewed by faulty or relatively unimportant assumptions. This principle then needs to be examined to see what it implies for the moral content of Scripture. Can we determine the distinctive heartbeat of the biblical message that also gives life and substance to the moral content of the Bible?

In the Reformation tradition going back to Martin Luther, the interpretive and organizing principle by which to understand the meaning of Scripture is christological. This means that the center of Scripture from which the whole biblical story is understood is the gospel of Jesus Christ. Of course, this hermeneutical principle cannot be applied in a heavy-handed manner so that we fail to appreciate the genuinely historical character of Scripture with all of its rough edges. Rightly applied, however, it provides the Christian with a focus that reveals the direction and goal of the biblical story. This christological principle, revealing God's love as the moving power in the world, serves us as well in understanding the moral authority of Scripture. In terms of the five approaches to the use of Scripture noted above, it places us particularly in the fourth approach, which recognizes the Bible's central message—the gospel of Jesus Christ—as foundational for the Christian life and yet at the same time recognizes that the particular heritage of one's church will contribute to the way one hears the meaning and application of that message for the moral life. The christological principle should not be used in an exclusive manner that prevents us, for example, from drawing the moral directions implicit in a Trinitarian approach (as noted in the third of the five approaches we discussed). It is the centerpiece, however, that promises the most fruitful avenue into the meaning of Scripture for the moral life.

The Commandment of Jesus to Love

The Christian understanding of God is shaped by the story of Jesus Christ, whose life embodies the divine love in human history. Jesus is not only God's gift and therefore the historical embodiment and presence of divine love; Jesus was also a rabbi (teacher) and in his teachings places love at the center of our relationships with both God and our neighbor. The importance of love as that which undergirds the whole moral life is clearly seen in Jesus' teaching from the incident involving the lawyer who came to him with a question:

> "Teacher, which is the great commandment in the law?" And he said to him, "You shall love the Lord your God with all your heart, and with all your soul, and with all your mind. This is the great and first commandment. And a second is like it, You shall love your neighbor as yourself." (Matt. 22:36-39; cf. Mark 12:28-31)

Though some would resist any attempt to capture the thrust of the Christian life in one concept, there is good reason to place self-giving love at its center.[3] The Gospel of John relates the love commandment to the pattern of Jesus' own life: "A new commandment I give to you, that you love one another; even as I have loved you, that you also love one another" (John 13:34). The whole meaning of Jesus and his message is expressed in love that reaches out in self-sacrificial action. A few passages from the Sermon on the Mount will make this clear in regard to Jesus' own teachings.

What Jesus says about the moral life in that material we call the Sermon on the Mount appears so radical in its demands that one is tempted to discount what he says. Indeed, he has been accused of irrelevance in view of words like these:

> You have heard that it was said, "An eye for an eye and a tooth for a tooth." But I say to you, Do not resist one who is evil. But if any one strikes you on the right cheek, turn to him the other also; and if any one would sue you and take your coat, let him have your cloak as well; and if any one forces you to go one mile, go with him two miles. Give to him who begs from you, and do not refuse him who would borrow from you. (Matt. 5:38-42)

Jesus' teaching envisions the breaking in of the kingdom of God; the rule and presence of God will create a new order in which righteousness prevails. Jesus' followers were now called to act as participants in the new order, for nothing else really mattered in light of the coming kingdom. The impact of the kingdom for Jesus' teaching is to direct us to our neighbor in radical fashion. Now no one's life impinges upon us more decisively than that neighbor who is in need. All other relations and obligations fade away as the end times relate us absolutely to that one neighbor.[4] Jesus places us in one-to-one fashion with the neighbor in need, and everything else becomes irrelevant in light of the primary imperative to answer that need.

Jesus also redefines the neighbor for us, sharpening and expanding our responsibility:

> You have heard that it was said, "You shall love your neighbor and hate your enemy." But I say to you, Love your enemies and pray for those who persecute you, so that you may be [children] of your Father who is in heaven; for he makes his sun rise on the evil and on the good and sends rain on the just and on the unjust. For if you love those who love you, what reward have you? Do not even the tax collectors do the same? And if you salute only your brethren, what more are you doing than others? Do not even the Gentiles do the same? You, therefore, must be perfect, as your heavenly Father is perfect. (Matt. 5:43-48)

Clearly, Jesus expects more from his followers than what the world of prudential wisdom leads us to expect from each other. Social morality reflects our concern to protect ourselves from those who are not willing to respect us and who may even want to take advantage of us. Thus, rules and laws take the form of prohibitions telling us what we ought *not* to do in case we are thinking of doing it. We are required to do no more than refrain from doing harm, recognizing the rights of our neighbors as we expect them to recognize ours. Jesus challenges us to move beyond this way of thinking, which is basically centered on our own claims to life and property. The imperative to love challenges us to move in positive, life-giving directions that reflect the goodness of God. Love seeks the welfare of the neighbor. Rather than dividing up our neighbors into friends and enemies, the spirit of agapeic love can even turn the enemy into our friend and thereby create a new world marked by reconciliation.

When we speak of love as the central concept in describing the ethical message of Jesus, as well as capturing most adequately the character of his own life story, we mean an authentic concern for the welfare of our neighbor. Without respect to whether one's neighbor is a friend, an enemy, or totally anonymous, if that person is in need of us we are called to respond to that need. The power of love is that it is no respecter of persons; love reaches out to whoever gives evidence of needing us, without asking embarrassing questions or imposing requirements.

This imperative to love will always impress us as extreme, for we do in fact define our moral obligations in what we might describe as concentric circles. The smallest, inner circle of people to whom we feel the greatest sense of obligation and moral responsibility is likely our immediate family. Beyond that circle may come our closest friends and then perhaps our associates at work or members of our church with whom we have shared our lives in a meaningful way. At the outermost edge would be the stranger. While these differences in our experience of obligation to others are understandable, the spirit of Jesus' teaching would prevent us from absolutizing these circles of responsibility and closing ourselves to the stranger or to whomever the circumstances of life might place on our doorstep. The imperative to love keeps us alive to the plight of the vulnerable, the person without friends and support. To love is to be open to need where others would not even recognize it—or allow themselves to recognize it.

The power and seriousness of Jesus' teaching for the Christian is rooted in the fact that he not only taught us to love but embodied that love in his own life. Saint Paul and other biblical writers recognize in the resurrected one a person in whom love gains its fullest expression, a love rooted in God and expressing the very nature of God as love. Paul consequently points to Jesus as both the embodiment of God's good news and the example for those who would live the God-pleasing life:

> Have this mind among yourselves, which you have in Christ Jesus, who, though he was in the form of God, did not count equality with God a thing to be grasped, but emptied himself, taking the form of a servant, being born in the likeness of [human

beings]. And being found in human form he humbled himself and became obedient unto death, even death on a cross. (Phil. 2:5-8)

When we point to self-giving love as the center of the Christian life, we are not talking about ethics alone. Christians believe that love is at the center of the universe in that God is love. They also believe, with Saint Paul, that Jesus is God's anointed one (the Christ) who reveals and carries out the divine mission of love. The above passage from Paul's letter to the Philippians reveals the close connection between Christian ethics and Christian theology. The imperative to love is based on the indicative that God *is* love. To tend to our neighbor is not only the God-pleasing thing; it is to do the God-like thing. This truth is expressed quite forcefully in the Johannine letters:

Beloved, let us love one another; for love is of God, and he who loves is born of God and knows God. He who does not love does not know God; for God is love. In this the love of God was made manifest among us, that God sent his only Son into the world, so that we might live through him. In this is love, not that we loved God but that he loved us and sent his Son to be the expiation for our sins. Beloved, if God so loved us, we also ought to love one another. No [one] has ever seen God; if we love one another, God abides in us and his love is perfected in us. (1 John 4:7-12)

Love and Making Moral Decisions

What does this exalted ideal of love really mean for us who are involved in the nitty-gritty of daily life, often confronted by situations that challenge us with shades of gray rather than obvious black-and-white decisions? We should note first that Jesus' teachings do not give much specific direction; his words about love do not make any kind of moral handbook. He does not satisfy our desire for moral absolutes in the form of laws that make it clear what we are *not* to do. While an occasional directive is recorded by the biblical writers (it is clear, for example, that divorce is contrary to God's intent), our desire for clear and concise answers to every moral problem or issue is not satisfied by his teachings.

What Jesus does give us is a vision of the God of love and what this vision means for our relationships with others. The central question becomes our relation to God; for Jesus, the kingdom of God is decisive in ordering the character and direction of our lives, which makes faith or trust in God the decisive factor for the moral life. Loving God and loving our neighbor are causally connected—to love God is to love (serve) our neighbor. Rather than give us a prescription, Jesus places us in the presence of the sovereign God whose power is love and who invites us (and necessarily challenges us) to demonstrate that power in the way we relate to our neighbors.

A distance still remains, however, between the Christian's trust in God as sovereign love and the concrete moral decisions the Christian makes. We might put it this way: Faith in God creates a disposition toward life and one's neighbor(s) that nurtures and encourages works of love. This underlying orientation sensitizes us to the condition of our neighbor but does not dictate the appropriate action. We are addressed by the imperative to love as people who trust in the God who is love. But what shape and form our love should take on behalf of our neighbor is something we have to figure out ourselves, with the support of our Christian community.

This situation of the Christian leads us to observe that *love and freedom together* best get at the nature of the Christian life. The Scriptures are clearly addressing people for whom something profound has happened: they have been claimed, overpowered, by the good news of God's acceptance of the sinner. Their lives are forgiven and therefore renewed; the past, which threatens them as a burden, has been wiped away through repentance and forgiveness. The freedom bestowed by this experience—relived throughout one's life—now characterizes the Christian's attitudes and outlook. The challenge now is to live as a person of faith, exercising one's freedom in constructive and responsible ways according to the mind of Christ. Two more passages from Paul are helpful in capturing this character of the Christian's life:

> Do not be conformed to this world, but be transformed by the renewal of your mind, that you may prove what is the will of God, what is good and acceptable and perfect. (Rom. 12:2)

Finally [brothers and sisters], whatever is true, whatever is honorable, whatever is just, whatever is pure, whatever is lovely, whatever is gracious, if there is any excellence, if there is anything worthy of praise, think about these things. (Phil. 4:8)

Our discussion to this point likely impresses many readers as being extremely idealistic. Can we really love our neighbor in the selfless, self-giving manner that the story of Jesus Christ would inspire? Moreover, quite apart from the possibility of our acting in this way, is it actually desirable? Is it not an invitation to masochism to continually "turn the other cheek"? Some would say it is utterly unrealistic to suppose that human beings can love without expecting something in return, for mutuality and reciprocity are fundamental to our relationships. Others argue that the idealization of selfless love fails to recognize the importance of self-love (or self-esteem), which is essential to our capacity to reach out to others in love.

Responding first to this last concern, note that Jesus himself assumed self-love—or an understandable concern for one's own welfare—to be present in the Christian life. This is reflected in the words "You shall love your neighbor as yourself." The point is not that we are to love our neighbor instead of ourselves but that our concern for self should not prevent us from reaching out to others. Those who do not care for themselves are clearly in trouble and need help. Jesus is not addressing that circumstance, but is simply recognizing that self-love is a reality that ought not stand in the way of loving our neighbor. To give of ourselves to another is always a challenge that requires personal strength and confidence. It will not happen, however, as long as we are unwilling to forget ourselves and tend to our neighbor.

Our relations to others are generally marked by mutuality and reciprocity. But at the same time, we cannot overlook the challenge to go beyond what is expected—this marks every ideal. The radical self-giving pictured in the Christian message does not fall within the comfortable expectations of a relationship marked by reciprocity. The ethics of love in Jesus' teaching and embodied in his life stands as a continuing challenge over all of history precisely because it pushes us further than we want to go. Its radical demand functions most often in the Christian life as a self-critical principle, compelling us to place our whole lives—our attitudes as well as our actions—under the light of its uncompromising demand. Christians grow by reaching beyond themselves. In the midst of all the competing drives, desires, and demands experienced in the day-to-day life of the Christian, the imperative to act in a spirit of love brings a more exalted focus to the Christian's life. It reminds us of our calling and challenges us, in a spirit of gratitude, to be faithful to that calling.

Let us return for a moment to our young couples, John and Blanche and Fred and Tina. In discussing their encounter, we noted some of the factors that lead to different life-styles, attitudes, and judgments found among Christians concerning social issues: ambiguities in moral and social issues themselves, the impact of one's church and its tradition, one's economic class, and one's education. Their encounter raised for us the question of whether any such thing as a Christian way of life is identifiable in the personal lives of Christians and in their approach to controversial issues in society. Now that we have considered the ethics of love, which we identified as inherent to the teaching of Jesus and the gospel proclaimed by the church, we can say more in responding to this question.

We see that the very nature of the life we are invited to live in Jesus' teaching is not one that finds expression primarily in laws and rules, important and necessary as they are. Jesus invites—and challenges—his disciples to live a life that goes beyond the law, a life of response to the goodness of God expressed in loving one's neighbor. We have no blueprint for action in every circumstance but an imperative to reach out in compassion to our neighbor in need, just as Jesus Christ has reached us in the good news of God's acceptance of the sinner.

In addition to this open-ended character of the imperative to love, which accentuates our freedom in Christ, there is also the fact that this message of love is also filtered through the personality and life history of the individual Christian. The imperative to love is subject to the possibilities allowed by the individual or expanded by the seriousness of the Christian's faith commitment, by the strengths and weaknesses of the individual's character, by the imagination brought to the situation, and by one's capacity for moral discernment and discrimination. All these factors can result in differences and disagreements among Christians on how to act in any given situation. What we would expect to find in every Christian, however, is the awareness that God is summoning him or her to a loving response in this situation. We would expect that Christians would recognize that on every occasion marked by a moral challenge, the ethics of the gospel summons one to act in a way that serves the welfare of the neighbor.

It is important to emphasize the point we have made: The *imperative* to love is rooted in the *indicative* of God's love of the sinner. Despite a variety of Christian experience also at this point, no Christian is likely to deny that recognition of God's love is an existential matter. It involves owning up to our inadequacies, our self-centeredness; it involves repentance for sin and the experience of God's forgiveness with its life-renewing power. This personal, experiential basis for the Christian life also brings its transforming impact. The Christian experience of conversion and renewal has led to profound changes in people's attitudes toward others and their willingness to become involved in works of love.

For John and Blanche, the imperative to love has taken on particular meaning and urgency in regard to social issues. Their concern for the welfare of the neighbor is expressed in their concern for justice for all people. Much of the excitement and power of the Christian message is found for them in the realm of social justice. Fred and Tina tend to understand the imperative to love within the context of evangelism, a love of the sinner and a desire that everyone find the abundant life in Christ. They are impressed with the many variables that enter into one's judgments on social issues, and, rather than bring these issues into the focus of the church's concern, they would leave them at the doorstep of the individual Christian. Christian ethics then becomes a consideration of the individual Christian's moral behavior. These two viewpoints are commonly found in every church, and we will return to this issue in a later chapter. Here we simply note the need to keep both personal and social morality within the proper concern of the church. It is good for the

Christian community as a whole that *both* of these couples are a part of the church!

In this chapter, we have considered the Bible as an authority and a resource for moral decision making and have focused on self-giving love as the biblical foundation for the Christian moral life. The gospel proclaimed in Scripture opens the possibility of trust in God, whose love of the sinner is a source of freedom and hope. This theological foundation gives focus and unity to the Christian understanding of the moral life. In spite of their differences, Christians would claim a common ideal and source of power rooted in the gospel message of divine love. To place love at the center of the Christian life means that making moral decisions is, first of all, a matter of *who* we are in terms of our religious and moral convictions. Being grasped by the love of God in Christ is relevant to the kind of moral person one is. It provides a common ground for Christians and a source of critique for their approach to moral decision making, even if it does not ensure a common answer to every moral problem.

FROM CONVICTIONS TO DECISIONS

Our examination of the Bible as a moral authority led us to recognize that self-giving love is central to the Christian view of the moral life. Making that point, however, does not give us specific directions for what to do in particular situations. This has been a common complaint about ethics in the Protestant tradition; we speak of loving our neighbor and tend to let it go at that. Roman Catholic moral tradition has always been more specific about what we ought to do in particular circumstances, but the help this can give to the individual also carries considerable risk. When the church gives the impression that it has a directive for every serious moral question we face, it encourages both legalism (preoccupation with laws or rules as the final answers to moral decision making) and a questionable dependence of the individual upon the institution of the church. This dependence is apt to become an obstacle rather than an aid to the development of one's moral responsibility. Rather than prescribe the answers to anticipated situations and provide moral handbooks for their members, churches perform a more meaningful service by helping their members to understand those imperatives and ideals by which they want to live as Christians, as well as by helping them focus on the elements of decision making.

When we place self-giving love at the heart of the Christian life, we address the foundational level of Christian ethics.[1] It is the point of beginning, before we get to concrete decisions. We acknowledge that to speak of moral decision making is, first of all, to recognize that acting morally involves a person's convictions about the meaning of life, the purpose of human existence, and what this means for the way we relate to other human beings. We can neither isolate our decisions from the particular circumstances in which they occur nor abstract the individual from moral decisions and discuss those decisions apart from the agent who makes them. *Who* one is determines whether one will likely act responsibly in the decisions one makes. In other words, making moral decisions confronts us immediately with issues of moral character and personal virtue.

Moral Character and the Decisions One Makes

Several ethicists in recent years have emphasized the importance of character and personal virtue to any consideration of ethics.[2] They have accused those working in the discipline of ethics of being too absorbed with decision making apart from the person who is making the decision. Rather than always asking, What ought I to do? the question is really, What ought I to be? or more accurately, What ought *we* to be? because the individual cannot be isolated from the community any more than the act can be isolated from the larger context in which it occurs. When ethics concentrates on the act of individual decision, it risks overlooking the importance of moral formation and those qualities of the individual essential to responsible, moral living. This becomes all the more critical in an age when Christian formation as a task for the family and church is not reinforced in the culture as in past generations.

An ethics of virtue, in contrast to an ethics of decision, stresses the priority of one's character over the decisions one makes. One's character shapes the way one sizes up the moral situation and how one arrives at a decision; it largely determines the decision that is made. While one's character may be confirmed by one's decisions, decisions do not determine character. Rather, character emerges from the convictions and dispositions that are rooted in one's life.[3]

Stanley Hauerwas, in arguing for an ethics of virtue, also maintains that the traditional way of doing ethics misleads us into thinking that we can establish universal standards for our moral decisions. By treating the act or decision as though it were an event unto itself, we are encouraged to think that the reasons we give for our moral decisions are objective standards untouched by historical change. This kind of objective basis is appealing to us in the midst of all the ambiguities of moral practice, but Hauerwas labels the quest for objectivity as rationalism that is less than truthful. Our standards are actually abstractions gleaned from reflecting on our life stories, and if we are honest we will acknowledge that whatever standards we come up with are rooted in those stories rather than some objective realm of universal truth.[4] The alternative is not subjectivism but the recognition that our moral lives are rooted in and inspired by stories or narratives of communities that have played a decisive role in shaping and directing our lives. Rather than insisting on objective absolutes that are immune to change, we should recognize that the imperatives by which we live are embedded in the social fabric and are known and experienced within a particular context that is meaningful for our lives. As we have noted, this context for the Christian is the community of faith that is rooted in the biblical revelation.

Posing an ethics of virtue against an ethics of decision has its dangers, however, if we are led to conclude that they are exclusive alternatives. Ethicists generally have recognized the importance of the subject or agent in moral action. The moral quality of an act cannot be grasped apart from the person doing it, with an understanding of the person's life story, perceptions of reality, motivations, and intentions. We are interested here in the dynamics and circumstances of moral decision making, but we have also recognized in the first two chapters that who we are in terms of our religious heritage and convictions is important to what we decide to do. By focusing first on the theological convictions of Christians, we have acknowledged that those beliefs that help to define us as human beings have a bearing on our moral life. If we seriously believe that God is love and self-giving is central in our relation to the neighbor, that conviction will contribute to the shaping of our disposition and outlook; we will take seriously the imperative to reach out to the neighbor. Specific answers to specific situations may not emerge with the clarity we desire, but an orientation develops that helps to generate our moral response.

The focus upon the subjective story of the individual as essential to understanding the world of ethics brings to mind the writings of the nineteenth-century religious thinker Søren Kierkegaard.[5] This enigmatic thinker, the father of twentieth-century existentialism, portrayed several life orientations—aesthetic, ethical, religious, and Christian—by depicting people who reflect in their lives the characteristics of each of these "stages on life's way." The meaning of the moral life is presented in the depiction of a judge by the name of Williams who is the very embodiment of moral integrity. Kierkegaard is not interested in what Judge Williams would decide concerning each of the moral issues of his time, but he is interested in the nature and quality of that life ruled by an ethical principle. Ethical people are inner-directed, revealing a fundamental stance in relation to the world. They seek to express the universal in their lives and the realization of their humanity through principled living.

What impressed Kierkegaard is that one cannot speak of the moral self, or of character and virtue, without noting the reality of moral failure. No matter how noble one's character, wholeness and integrity remain beyond reach. He concludes that the highest expression of the moral life is ultimately repentance, and yet that option is not open to the person whose life is governed by moral categories; it is, rather, a religious possibility. Thus, Kierkegaard finds a Christian reading of life experience to reveal a more profound possibility for wholeness of self: repentance and forgiveness. We find ourselves not through the attainment of moral perfection but through recognizing our failure and embracing the forgiveness offered in the gospel. This consciousness of human sin and divine grace is at the center of Christian self-consciousness and helps the Christian avoid the temptation of thinking that ethics is the means toward attaining moral perfection. Precisely as moral agent, or moral decision maker, the Christian trusts in the grace of God.

Love and Law in the Christian Life

An important feature of a Christian's moral character is the interplay of love and law in that person's attitudes toward the moral life and in his or her own self-consciousness as a child of God. We have described the Christian life in terms of love and freedom, in contrast to an ethics based simply on law. We have noted that love invites a response that goes beyond the law, even as law remains important to one's moral life. When we address our decision making, more needs to be said about the relation of love and law because it is, in fact, a rather complicated subject.

The relation of love to law has been a perennial issue among Christians. In recent times, that issue has come most clearly to expression in the situation ethics debate, and it might be helpful to approach this subject within the context of that debate.[6] Those flying the banner of situation ethics are impressed by the dominance of law in traditional ethics and argue (as we have also) that love and freedom express the real essence of Christian ethics, if one is to be faithful to the teachings of both Jesus and Paul. They also point to the legalism in many Christian communities and in the thinking of too many individual Christians as evidence that we have failed as a church to communicate the distinctive character of the Christian life. Not law, but love is at the center of Christian ethics and the Christian life.

Most of us will appreciate the attempt to recover the centrality of love in Christian ethics, and we will also most likely deplore the legalism too often apparent in Christian communities. However, some situationists give the impression that we are faced with an either/or: it is either love or law, and if love is central there is no place for law. This view is seen in Joseph Fletcher's work, where law is replaced by principles that are defined as moral wisdom serving as guidelines.[7] He rejects the use of rules or any kind of imperative that lays claim to being absolute and universal. Emphasizing the uniqueness of each moral situation, Fletcher cannot see the truth or usefulness of any rule or law that claims to express a moral order that ought not be broken. The only absolute in every situation is to love.

Fletcher argues his case by presenting situations in which the most fundamental and universal rule begs to be broken. Take, for example, the Ten Commandments. Most of us would not want to challenge those commandments that tell us not to steal, not to commit adultery, or not to speak falsely. Nonetheless, Fletcher maintains the situation may sometimes command us to transgress these absolutes and go ahead and steal (if one is poverty-stricken and faced with starvation) or commit adultery (if one is imprisoned and cannot gain release by the guard without first submitting to him) or lie (if it is necessary to save someone from being destroyed). He concludes that love and the situation are to determine our behavior, not law.

Without question, the situation will have a bearing on what we decide is morally fitting behavior. A major problem for Christian ethics is getting straight the relation between the situation and those moral imperatives that undergird our society and that we acknowledge as expressions of divine will. The more universal these imperatives or laws appear to us, the more fundamental they are in maintaining a protective order necessary for a society's moral life. The Ten Commandments have carried this authority in Western society, with the first table of the commandments (referring to God's sovereignty and our worship of God) giving explicit expression to their divine origin and the second table providing a moral framework for a number of fundamental human relationships. We appropriately identify this ordering and protecting function of law with the will and command of God. It provides the framework for responsible living before God and the community, but this does not deny the fact that in unusual circumstances we may find it necessary to suspend the law's imperative. Fletcher's mistake is supposing that, because we can imagine situations in which it could be justifiable to transgress a law, the law therefore loses its validity as an expression of God's ordering will.

We don't have to insist, then, that God's law is absolutely unbreakable in order to maintain its indispensable function in the moral life. The "thou shalt nots" that protect society are needed because of our inclination to act in ways that are self-centered or self-serving. Law helps us recognize appropriate boundaries to the imposition of our will and interests upon others. No one gets beyond the need for hearing the accusing word and being challenged to examine one's motives and goals. Thus, law remains essential to the Christian life, even if it is not the distinguishing feature of Christian morality. That remains self-giving love, which will often move the Christian to do more than the law requires.

In their own way, both law and love seek the welfare of the neighbor. The law protects both the neighbor and myself from each other; it sets the proper boundaries to our relationships. Love is much more than this: it both abides by the law and goes beyond the law in acts of reconciliation and altruism that generate community. Christians can never be content with a law-based morality because it simply states the minimal requirements for civilized life. Love bears a creative power that changes the relationships between people and opens new possibilities for them.

We want to subordinate the law, then, without minimizing its importance or its necessity. People tend to emphasize the law when they get worried about the moral confusion that we have noted and when they sense an erosion of moral responsibility in society. This is a legitimate concern, for our awareness of moral obligation is a distinctly human experience that is essential to our humanity and to the welfare of society. The Ten Commandments and other fundamental expressions of law are important because they confront us with the ultimate worth of our fellow human beings, obligating us to respect them and to recognize—with the moral philosopher Immanuel Kant—that our neighbor is to be treated as an end, not as a means. Specific commandments express this truth about a number of fundamental relationships, such as those between husband and wife, between people and their property, between people in the legitimate quest for truth, and so on. Respect for these laws is respect for people.

We conclude that the Christian life is best understood as response to the gospel in a spirit of gratitude, but the law both orders our lives and keeps us accountable in our weakness. Law and love (reflecting the Christian message of law and gospel) are to be distinguished and contrasted with each other as well as to be recognized as complementary. The God of the gospel is also the God of the law; the God to whom we respond in faith and love of neighbor is the God who holds us accountable through the demands of life reflected in the laws and rules that govern our corporate life. We must recognize this two-sided character of demand and promise in Christian experience, rather than seek to resolve its tension. No matter how deeply rooted the faith or how profound the moral commitment, the reality of our fallenness is a constant reminder for the Christian of the reality of divine judgment as well as divine grace and forgiveness.

Acting by Duty and Ideal

The history of ethical theory reveals two major approaches to understanding the basis on which one makes a moral decision. One stresses the notion of duty and roots the right decision in our sense of obligation. When we act according to duty, which we are normally able to recognize as human beings, then we are doing what is right. This is the *deontological* view (referring to the concept of duty) in which rules and law play an important role. The second approach, called the *teleological* view (referring to a goal or purpose), stresses the ideals or goals of our decision making. This view roots the morally good action in the end or goal by which one acts. The language here is not that of law or rule but of a guiding ideal or value. In some situations, these two methods of moral decision making can appear to be in dramatic conflict with each other. Take, for example, the dilemma that confronted the young guerrilla fighter, Adolfo Lopez.

At the age of nineteen, Adolfo Lopez moved out of his parents' home and joined a partisan uprising. It was a decision prompted both by cruel necessity as well as by intense patriotism. When a group of army officers overthrew the civilian government, his father was imprisoned, and Adolfo's family soon heard reports that his father and other government figures were being tortured. The new government imposed martial law and quickly exercised totalitarian control. Young Adolfo believed he was in danger of imprisonment himself because of his political activities at the university. The resistance movement was led by military and civilian leaders who were committed to democratic ideals and who vowed to fight for a government that would truly be representative of the people. It was not long before Adolfo's guerrilla unit was involved with government forces in a skirmish in which a high-ranking army officer was captured by the partisans. They quickly recognized that this man possessed highly sensitive information concerning the strategic planning of the government forces. To get that knowledge was crucial for the success of the partisan cause.

Adolfo was part of a contingent guarding the officer, and he witnessed hours of intense grilling that could not extract the needed information. Finally, they decided the man must be tortured if they were to be successful. Adolfo was given orders to apply a red hot branding iron to the officer's body until he talked.

Can an act of torture be morally justified? To say that it can means the goal or end purpose of the act is seen as such an important moral value that it actually justifies a means that one would otherwise reject. This is a teleological argument, based on a good or a value that one seeks to realize. In the case of Adolfo, if torturing the officer results in information that enables the partisans to overthrow a totalitarian government and liberate hundreds of prisoners, many of whom are being tortured, then one may argue that the act was morally acceptable.

In contrast to this view, a deontological perspective would maintain that torture is an evil that is never made morally acceptable by its consequences. Whether it is assaulting someone with a branding iron, dropping the atomic bomb on Hiroshima in order to hasten the end of a dreadful war, or deceiving one's neighbor in order to protect her from hearing some very bad news, the end purpose or goal of the act does not make right what is intrinsically wrong. The deontologist will also point out that any attempt to determine the end result of one's action is not only difficult but impossible—often presenting a two-edged sword. Assuming the teleological argument in the case of Adolfo, torturing someone may achieve one goal but also result in other, unintended results that seriously compromise the intended good. To torture an enemy captive is to invite similar tactics from the enemy, with yet more wanton disregard for life and an evil intensification of the conflict. One can also question whether practicing such a degrading evil as human torture is not destructive of one's own humanity or the moral fabric of one's life. Can one, in fact, so neatly divide the end from the means?

Our discussion of this incident reveals the differing context for deontological and teleological ethics. The former recognizes our need of rules and law, which would restrict our inclination to do evil. The latter lifts up a goal or ideal to which we can commit ourselves. Both emphases are clearly needed, for we are capable of both evil and good. The deontological view becomes extraordinarily important in times when we are tempted to rationalize our way out of a difficult moral obligation. In such moments, we pass through the crucible of moral struggle, a testing of character to hold to what is right simply because it is right or to reject what is wrong simply because it is wrong. In this case, the immorality of torture should compel Adolfo to resist committing the act, even as a guerrilla engaged in warfare.[8]

On the other hand, we will often find ourselves in more benign situations in which we are attempting to figure out what would be the best thing to do in serving our neighbor. In these circumstances, we will try to assess the outcome of different courses of action; it is not a matter of what ought I not to do but rather, given the limitations of the situation, what may be the best thing to do in serving my neighbor. My desire to fulfill that purpose will keep me honest with myself, and the experience does not involve a serious wrestling with temptation. The goal itself is too important to me. Here one is thinking in the teleological mode.

Some would identify the Christian ethics of love with a teleological approach, but this fails to see the continuing importance of law in the Christian's life. We see both law and love as motivating factors: the law challenges us to be faithful and judges our self-serving actions, and love moves us to act on behalf of the neighbor's welfare. To act in love can also be experienced and expressed in the language of command ("Love your neighbor as yourself"), for the follower of Christ whose moral sensitivities have been formed by the Christian message will recognize the imperative force of exercising concern for the welfare of the neighbor. Because the gospel exalts each person as a child of God and the object of divine love, the responsibility of the believer to the neighbor is heightened. Thus, love leads us beyond the command of the law at the same time as it is experienced as a command by the follower of Christ. It challenges us to go the second mile.

We have referred to law (duty) and love (seeking the welfare of one's neighbor) as motives of moral action. But of course, a variety of motives may actually enter into our moral decisions and actions. Christians are particularly sensitive to the importance of motive, for it relates to the inner life of character and one's relationship to God, who knows the heart. We recognize and lament our capacity to act in self-serving and devious ways even when achieving an end result that may be helpful and good for any number of people. Whatever the end result, however, the good or genuine motive is essential to the moral quality of what one does, whether acting from a sense of duty that affirms one's personal integrity or from a single-minded desire to do all one can in serving the welfare of one's neighbor. Unfortunately, one can earnestly desire the welfare of another and yet act in a way that actually obstructs rather than effects the intended good (a matter to be discussed in the next section). For this reason our concern about moral decision making goes well beyond a consideration of the motive alone, without denying its central importance to the moral character of any act. If we understand our moral life as our response to God and God's creation, our motivations become an integral part of the responsible life.

The term *response* suggests a theologian who has proposed an alternative to deontological and teleological thinking. H. Richard Niebuhr focuses on the agent who is making the moral decision, whom Niebuhr understands as a creature in a state of response to the Creator. The challenge of life, which conveys the challenge of God, is that one *responds* in a way that is *responsible*. As people living in community, Niebuhr maintains that we live "less under universal law and less in pursuit of a universal ideal than a life of responsibility in universal community."[9] Rather than speak of law and ideal, he describes responsible action as "fitting" and relates what is fitting not only to the situation but ultimately to the whole story of our lives lived in relation to the Christian story of creation and redemption. While we will want to retain the language of duty and ideal, the particularly appealing feature of Niebuhr's ethics of responsibility is that it places us in the presence of God, giving both an ethical and theological meaning to the responsible life.

Responsibility is such an important concept to the moral life that we must add it as the third term in the triad of *freedom, love, and responsibility* that describes the Christian life. It adds the recognition that God holds us to account in the many demands of life that challenge us to respond in faithful living. The motivation to love one's neighbor is centered in the gospel, but the fallenness of our lives will often turn the loving response into a challenge and a burdensome command. Responsibility captures the note of obligation that always marks the moral life and that for the Christian centers ultimately in the command to love one's neighbor. These three concepts have an abstract character about them, but understood within the context created by the Christian message, they provide a framework that captures the nature of the Christian life. In the freedom bestowed by forgiveness, Christians can act in a spirit of gratitude on behalf of their neighbor's welfare, recognizing that this is both their opportunity as well as their responsibility to God and to their neighbor.

Discerning What I Ought to Do

One can understand the centrality of love and the importance of law to Christian ethics and still be rather ineffective in sizing up the moral situation and making the fitting decision. Here one can speak of discernment as an important attribute in moral decision making. By discernment we mean the capacity to exercise discriminating judgment in making decisions, getting to the core of an issue by cutting through elements of self-interest that skew one's judgments. It involves honesty with oneself and with others. We can be well meaning and well intentioned, but in given situations we can display "blind spots" that warp our capacity for responsible moral judgment. The dynamics of the situation may hinder our moral discernment. The case of Robert and Carla Mitchell illustrates the problem.

It would be difficult to find a more beautiful couple than Robert and Carla. They are devoted to each other and to their friends; they are highly respected both in their church and their community. They are often asked to assume positions of leadership at Trinity Episcopal Church because of their willingness to tackle challenging tasks and the good spirit they bring to these assignments.

Seventeen years ago, the Mitchells, who were childless, became the guardians of Jimmy, a one-year-old whose parents had abandoned him. Within a year they had legally adopted Jimmy, and they raised him as typically doting parents would. He was their only child and was showered with the attention affluent parents can offer a single child. They were deeply moved by a desire to make Jimmy happy, perhaps affected particularly by the fact that he had been rejected by his own parents. As he grew up, Jimmy was told of the circumstances by which he became the Mitchells' child. His sense of being "special" as one who was chosen by his new parents was driven home to Jimmy both by word and by the often extravagant care given to him.

During his adolescent years, Jimmy began to exhibit the usual signs of growing independence. What began to trouble family friends, however, were the acts of disrespect to his parents that exceeded the usual boundaries of careless teenage behavior. He began to stay away overnight without telling his parents where he was; he engaged in acts of petty theft; he embarrassed the Mitchells rather often with intentionally obnoxious behavior. Robert and Carla were inclined to excuse these incidents as understandable signs of growing up, a "stage" in his life they would have to endure. Deeper alienation continued to develop, however, with Jimmy leaving home prior to his eighteenth birthday. A few weeks later, he was arrested on a charge of burglary. Court proceedings revealed that he had been burglarizing for several months in order to maintain a drug habit that had developed during the past year.

Many parents, like the Mitchells, have found themselves asking the question, What went wrong? Of course, particular dynamics are at work in a parent-child relationship that can complicate the process of discernment. But whatever the context, each personal relationship bears moral dimensions that challenge people to make astute moral judgments as well as to act on them. The Mitchells would have been helped in their rearing of Jimmy if they had been able to understand their intense desire to bring him happiness. It was a natural desire, but happiness itself is never a sufficient goal in life without its being subjected to moral examination. In Jimmy's case, happiness was understood as receiving an abundance of good things that gladden the heart of a boy growing up. But happiness so defined was experienced and understood by Jimmy as something the world owed him.

The ability to discern what is morally appropriate is indispensable to any desire to love one's neighbor. The Mitchells cannot be faulted on their desire to love Jimmy. But *how* to love or *how* to seek what is best for one's neighbor requires the capacity to know one's neighbor and to make the often hard decisions that best serve his or her welfare. The centrality of love in Christian ethics should not mislead one to suppose that Christians are not to exercise judgment and challenge the neighbor, for that can also be motivated by love or concern for the neighbor's welfare. This reminds us that situations demanding our moral judgments often require us to act courageously as well. The Mitchells, for whatever psychological reasons, were unwilling to define Jimmy's welfare in ways that would require discipline at appropriate times or specific moral guidance that would challenge and shape emerging attitudes.

Several things can be mentioned concerning what goes into moral discernment. The Mitchells needed to know Jimmy exceedingly well, to observe his responses to life situations and to sense the directions of his own moral judgments and attitudes. They also needed to know themselves and the motivation at work in their own lives in relation to Jimmy, and to be sensitive to those factors that made them vulnerable to his wants and desires. Knowledge of the moral situation and of one's neighbor, as well as insight into oneself, are all relevant to responsible moral decision making. This can indeed be a complex matter, but no one ever suggested that making moral judgments was simple!

One might put it this way: making moral decisions is always more than being rightly motivated or acting according to a sense of obligation. It also involves sufficient knowledge of "the facts of the matter" to make one's decision truly fit the situation. Robert and Carla, despite their good intentions, failed to accurately read Jimmy's situation; for whatever reasons, they ignored certain developments taking place in his life and in their relationship to him that should have informed the way they conducted themselves. Sentiment and emotion were getting in the way of proper objectivity, preventing them from maintaining the distance needed to assess the situation and then to act upon it.

Another factor is the necessity of defining one's goals in a morally responsible way. We have noted that the Mitchells' view of Jimmy's happiness was superficial, lacking moral content. Happiness is an important dimension of anyone's life, but it is insufficient as an end in itself because it lacks content. People define happiness in many different ways, even in ways that are self-serving and ultimately self-destructive. Happiness can also be defined much more profoundly, in which it becomes the accompaniment of a life devoted to the service of others. This definition would make happiness the reward of giving rather than receiving. Happiness is gratefully experienced but does not serve us well as an end in itself. This is particularly pertinent in a time when a materialistic society exalts happiness as the goal of life and defines it in terms of what money can buy.

A more appropriate goal for Jimmy or for any human being would be a fully human life, a life that captures our sense of the God-given destiny inherent to being human. This would include the nurture and flowering of our God-given capacities, with the goal of bringing them to the service and welfare of the human community.

The Christian message has always inspired a service-oriented perspective that has contributed profoundly to the moral health of society. The recent impact of individualism in the sphere of religious experience has often led to centering one's attention on one's own religious development rather than on service to the community. This orientation fails to grasp the truth expressed by Jesus, that it is in giving that one receives (Luke 6:38). The highest "ideal" one can glean from Scripture is the kingdom of God, an eschatological symbol that would embrace the whole human family. Not only does it express our destiny as children of God, but it also inspires a life that brings reconciliation and builds community. The Christian life by its very nature is one that reaches out to others.

What About the Conscience?

The conscience has had a long and venerable history in both secular and Christian ethics. It expresses the idea that we are aware of what is right and wrong and find ourselves inwardly accused when we do something that we know is wrong. Saint Paul expresses this idea in Romans 2, where he discusses the Gentiles, who have the law's demands "written in their hearts" even though they do not possess the law of Moses. Their conscience "also bears witness" to what the law requires. The conscience is not referred to by Paul as the source of our knowledge of good and evil but reflects our capacity to know when we are in the wrong.

Sometimes people speak of the conscience as a moral faculty that either by intuition or by the power of reason knows immediately what is right and wrong in a universal and transcendent sense. This view is not helpful for us today because we are aware that all moral obligations, whatever the extent of their universality throughout the world, are learned within particular societies and reflect the moral traditions of those societies. This truth is reflected in H. Richard Niebuhr's comment, "Conscience is a function of my existence as a social being, always aware of the approvals and disapprovals of my action by my fellow men."[10] This means that conscience is shaped by the community in which one is raised, marked by its moral distinctions as well as its continuities with other human communities. The church itself has an important responsibility to shape the conscience of society by exalting self-giving love and by seeking to embody that love.

The conscience is testimony to the fact that we are moral beings for whom right and wrong, good and bad, are meaningful categories and essential to our personal identity as social beings. The accusing conscience is not to be written off as a vestige of another age that psychotherapy can dissolve for us by explaining it away. A person who is sick will need therapy, but the accusing conscience more often testifies to the reality of right and wrong conduct and to the importance of morality for all personal and social relationships. Morality is a constituting factor of our lives because we are beings-in-relationship, and relationships immediately introduce morality.

This view does not allow for the conscience to function as some automatic homing device that zeroes in to inform us what we are to do. We may have moments in addressing difficult moral decisions when we suddenly gain clarity about the situation and become convinced about what we should do, but there is nothing automatic about it, and it is less than helpful to ascribe such insight to some kind of moral faculty we call the conscience. There is no shortcut to the hard thinking—the exercise of discernment—that difficult situations require of us. We need accurate knowledge of the situation, application of moral convictions or principles, and the willingness to act on those convictions. We also often need considerable courage to make ourselves vulnerable in serving the welfare of our neighbor.

We might summarize our discussion of what goes into moral decisions by noting the following levels of influence and involvement in the individual's arrival at a decision:

Society Level	The individual nurtured and shaped by the social and cultural milieu—family, neighborhood, peer groups, schools, church.
Individual Level	The character of the individual developed over the years; the impact of the Christian story, of principles, ideals, values; capacities for moral discernment; conscience, moral courage.
Situation Level	The confrontation with a particular issue; knowledge of the situation and exercise of discernment; application of principles consonant with one's personal identity.

Distinguishing between these "levels" of activity is a theoretical exercise that helps us gain clarity on the elements of decision making. In actual practice, however, these levels merge into the concrete situation and are not easy to distinguish. They do reveal that the influences on moral behavior are complex and looking at the situation alone is inadequate in understanding the dynamics of our decision making. Whatever the complexity of our moral life, our moral choices do reveal who we really are. When we summon the courage to make a difficult decision, keeping our eye on the moral values involved rather than allowing self-interest or self-indulgence to determine the decision, we are making an eloquent statement about who we are. It is a reminder that every moral decision we make is a profound reflection of our personal identity. The different situations we often face in our day-to-day living provide the occasions for either growth and deepening or a weakening of our moral character.

In the next chapter we will pose some hypothetical situations that challenge our powers of discernment as well as our moral courage. They will not always suggest a clear answer on what one ought to do, but by placing ourselves in the situation we will be challenged to think through the grounds for the decisions we would make. That in itself will possibly provide an occasion for enhancing our own capacities for moral judgment.

FACING SOME MORAL DILEMMAS

In many areas of our common life we face moral issues that seem to defy clear and satisfying solutions. Some may argue that the more reflective and analytical we become about these moral dilemmas, the more destined we are to never reach satisfaction with the decisions we make. On the contrary, careful reflection and analysis contribute to our moral discernment and enable us to make more responsible choices. Equally important is the Christian's consciousness that God calls us to the responsible life and embraces us in love. This reality encourages us to act with confidence, even in those situations that do not seem to allow a clear-cut, fitting answer. This is what Luther had in mind when he exhorted his Christian friends to "sin boldly." Carefully discerning moral situations, and trusting in the forgiveness of God, the Christian is equipped to act with confidence even in the most difficult circumstances.

Christian Vocation and One's Employment

For most people, getting a job does not likely raise ethical questions. As long as one's work is legal, there is nothing more to think about. For the Christian, however, one's occupation or profession is seen within the broader scope of one's vocation as a disciple of Jesus Christ. This may or may not necessitate a visible change in a Christian's way of life. In the Protestant tradition, Christians have not regarded their discipleship as necessitating a radical departure from traditional life-styles; one can be faithful as a full participant in society rather than, for example, withdrawing to the desert to pursue a life of contemplation. One can marry, raise a family, and be successful in a lucrative profession while living responsibly as a person of faith.[1]

What, then, are questions that would be relevant to raise for a Christian in considering an occupation? In many respects, the questions Christians raise would be the same as for anyone else: Is this the kind of work for which I am suited in temperament, intelligence, and training? Is this work that I can enjoy and from which I can draw a sense of accomplishment and personal fulfillment? These kinds of personal questions are important to all of us because we tend to be wedded to a career for most of our lives; it demands our time and dedication during a large part of each working day.

In addition to these questions, however, the Christian would be interested to know how his or her occupation fits into the larger sense of vocation bestowed by the gospel. Does my occupation or profession give the satisfaction that I am contributing to a better world—however small and relatively insignificant that contribution might be? The world of business is the setting where many Christians raise this question, and often the rat-race mentality found in highly competitive fields can create problems for one's sense of vocation. Our first dilemma comes from the business world; we will consider possible resolutions and close with some reflections on business and Christian vocation.

Jerry Britt was bright, personable, and energetic. His four years of college had been a pleasant mixture of work and play, with enough work to land him on the dean's list during his last two years. Friends admired his capacity to enjoy a good time as well as his high moral standards and sense of fair play. His parents were devout Christians who wanted their only son to get a college education rather than to stay home and run the family farm. Mr. Britt had been running the farm since he was twenty-three years old, but he saw no future in it for Jerry and encouraged him to prepare for a profession that would be more promising.

During his sophomore year, Jerry got interested in some business courses and decided on a business major. He thought he had the gifts to be an effective salesperson and looked forward to the challenge of earning high commissions in a competitive field. He had particularly enjoyed the course "Business and Society" during his senior year, in which much discussion centered on case studies illustrating the moral challenges faced by people in business, including sales. He was confident he could handle any situation he might face.

Shortly before graduation, Jerry was interviewed by a representative of Norwalk Models, Ltd., a company located in Chicago that produced equipment for retail store displays. He visited the plant, liked the people and the working atmosphere, and decided to sign on. It looked like a good opportunity with an established company.

Six months into his job, Jerry was given a tremendous opportunity. A retail company had bought and renovated a large building not far from Norwalk and was preparing it for use. The potential in sales volume for Norwalk was enormous, and Jerry's boss, the sales manager, let him know that this client was terribly important to him. "This kind of opportunity doesn't come along every day or even every year," he said.

Jerry established a good relationship with the store's purchasing agent and before long had worked out a sizeable sales agreement. He was enthused over his success in beating out several competitors and could hardly contain his excitement as he and the purchasing agent sat down to close the deal. He would never forget what happened next.

The purchasing agent said she had enjoyed working with Jerry and that a friendly relationship was essential to striking a deal. It would be helpful to her, she continued, if Jerry would pad the Norwalk bill by $1,000, which would go into the pocket of the purchasing agent. She explained this as the usual practice in this business and said she was not asking for more than what any agent would expect. If Jerry was not willing to go along, the agent could always find another company and another salesperson who could take his place. Jerry tried to retain his composure as he asked for time to think it over. The two agreed to meet the next day either to close on the transaction or call it off.

Jerry returned to his boss and related the incident. To his surprise, his boss was not particularly upset. "We run into this off and on, particularly in certain kinds of retail business," he said. "It's part of the game, and I'm afraid we have to play along." Jerry was clearly uncomfortable and after observing him a few moments the sales manager leaned forward and spoke with an intensity that added to Jerry's distress. "Listen, Jerry," he said. "Business is not a game for weaklings. Whenever you deal with large sums of money, someone is going to get a piece of it. That's just part of the picture. This sale means an awful lot to Norwalk and a hell of a commission for you. Don't blow it for Norwalk or yourself!"

Jerry's position is made doubly difficult because it is not only a matter between him and the agent but between him and his own company. He has encountered a practice that ordinarily would be judged wrong and unacceptable. In the context of his particular business, however, it was justified both by the one who expected to have her pockets filled and by the one who had to fill them. What should Jerry do? We will enumerate some possible responses.

1. Jerry should not be regarded as responsible in this case. He is just the middle person between his company and the agent, and if both are open to indulging in this practice, then Jerry can do nothing but comply. At the most, he could decide for the future to turn over this company's account to another Norwalk salesperson.

2. A more radical response is called for. Jerry should refuse to return to the agent and request that the account be turned over to another salesperson to close the deal on behalf of Norwalk. This would be a much more significant act on Jerry's part, for he would also be giving up his commission. The moral impact of such an action would be considerable because a large sum of money was involved.

3. The above response is not sufficient in view of the moral seriousness of Jerry's situation. He should resign on the spot, telling his boss that, not only was he opposed to engaging in this kind of negotiation, he also refused to work for a company that was willing to play this kind of game. The impact of such a moral statement would be greater still in that, not only was a commission rejected, but a promising future with the company as well.

All of the above responses are similar in that they help Jerry avoid compromising himself with what he rightly perceived to be a morally unacceptable practice. They differ according to the degree to which he was willing to compromise himself with what was going on. There is, however, a different kind of response that can be argued:

4. Jerry should see this issue in larger terms than his own "purity"; he should fight back rather than walk out. He may or may not withdraw from this particular case, but he should do what he can to organize a response on the part of Norwalk that would challenge the practices of bribery and kickbacks as they exist in certain segments of that industry. He might approach his sales manager again and share his vision for the establishment of a code of ethics at Norwalk. Together they might approach the upper management of the company, or Jerry could ask his boss's permission to pursue the matter himself with the appropriate management person. He would have to marshal his arguments and give attention to matters of strategy. If he is successful in getting Norwalk and possibly also its major competitors to adopt a strong policy on this issue, it would not only improve the moral environment in which he was working but significantly enhance the image of his company and make a difference in the moral tone of the industry.

As we have noted, it is not possible to make responsible moral judgments without knowing all the relevant facts of a situation. For example, in anticipation of his commission, Jerry may have promised his distraught parents that he would pay the balance on their harvester to avoid its being repossessed. We might decide that, therefore, Jerry should proceed with the first response if it is the only way he can raise the needed money on time. It would be a decision based on expediency rather than principle, an act of compromise in which one chooses between two possibilities, neither of which is wholly right and good. From our discussion in the previous chapter, we recognize this as teleological reasoning, where one decides that the end goal justifies the means. If we proceed simply on the basis of what we are told in this incident, however, we can argue with good reason for the fourth response in which Jerry challenges a dishonest and destructive practice and seeks to ensure a more honest environment. His sense of responsibility goes beyond himself to embrace a larger vocation.

This does not deny that the second or third response may be the most fitting under certain circumstances. The fourth response lays upon Jerry the role of a reformer, and that mantle is not worn—nor can it be expected to be worn—by everyone. It calls for some outstanding gifts and qualities that not everyone has, but Jerry appears to be one who could think seriously about challenging the system. Christians, in any event, would want to do what they could to raise the moral quality of their working environment, however that could best be done. That kind of concern is essential to the health of society at large and reflects the proper concern of Christians for their community as well as for the quality of their own moral lives. The two are intimately connected.

How does this discussion of Jerry Britt's moral options relate to the understanding of Christian ethics as the response in love to the need of one's neighbor? In analyzing the situation, we noticed that Jerry feels obligated to refrain from compromising himself with dishonest conduct. This was an immediate and healthy response to wrongdoing, reflecting the impact of law and a sense of duty. The specifically Christian imperative leads one to go further and to ask, What now can I do in this situation for the welfare of my neighbor? That question has possibilities of change and reform in Jerry's case; it brings challenges that will test his moral and religious convictions. We could easily imagine that the imperative to love would bring him back to the purchasing agent to explain why he could not participate in this action and to share his concern for the industry. The agent would not likely appreciate or even understand what Jerry is talking about, but an important witness would be made and an evil directly confronted.

The hard-nosed rush for personal and corporate advancement and the cynicism it inspires has led many to lament that success in business demands throwing ethics out the window. This kind of response encourages Christians to avoid business as a profession lest they be compelled to forsake their personal integrity. A more likely result is that Christians will continue to enter the world of business but at the cost of departmentalizing their lives, accepting one kind of morality for the business world and another when they come home from work. Admittedly, the more competitive the environment and the higher the financial stakes, the greater the temptation to act to one's advantage at the expense of one's integrity. Because intense competition and lucrative financial rewards are common to business, we need highly principled people working in business to encourage and maintain high moral standards. The Christian instinct, unlike that of many religions, is not to avoid evil in order to save oneself but to enter the fray in order to change things, transforming an evil situation into a good one.

The church may sometimes give the impression that a Christian can best serve others through the so-called helping professions in which one is directly involved in extending services to people in physical or spiritual need. This view defines "physical or spiritual need" so narrowly that most business professions would not qualify as activities that "love your neighbor." This is unfortunate, for all business activity is involved in meeting the needs of people, and only where the end product is destructive of human welfare would a Christian want to avoid involvement.[2] We need Christians in business who express their vocation with intentionality precisely because of a highly competitive and challenging environment. They should serve as leaders in their insistence upon quality of product and responsible standards of conduct. There is ample evidence that companies with quality leadership and integrity will soon establish their reputation and gain the confidence of consumers.

Reassessing Homosexuality

The realm of sexuality likely generates more uncertainty and agitation among Christians and the rest of the population than any other area of our common life. Relations between the sexes seem to be in a state of flux as men and women attempt to forge new understandings of their roles in the family and the economic world. If the stability of the family is a major barometer of the health of society, it is no wonder that people are concerned over a growing divorce rate that in recent years has resulted in approximately one divorce for every two marriages occurring in our society.[3] Amid prophecies that family life as we have known it is doomed to disappear, an increasing number of young people have decided just to live together rather than to legalize their union. A further complication is the reassessment taking place both in church and society concerning homosexuality and the growing influence of gays and lesbians in pressing the cause of civil rights for homosexuals.

Reactions in the Christian community to these developments have been varied. Some Christians have been hostile and judgmental, while others have expressed cautious willingness at least to reexamine traditional positions. Still others have accepted many new developments as appropriate to new understandings and attitudes within a changing society. Christians are well advised neither to see every change as an invention of the devil nor as a prompting of the Spirit of God. Rather than reacting instinctively according to a conservative or liberal mind-set, the task for Christians is to examine with moral discrimination the changes taking place, raising questions that will shed light on the reasons for change and the impact those changes will have on the moral health of society. This means the resources of the social sciences as well as the church's tradition must be employed to gain understanding and develop perspective on the changing scene.

Developments in the area of homosexuality deserve particular attention on the part of the Christian community. Incidents like the following are occurring with increasing frequency throughout the church, posing some very important and challenging questions.

St. John Lutheran Church had an active men's club that occasionally sponsored events for the whole congregation. These events were generally educational, featuring films or speakers on a topic of current interest. What the club had scheduled for its October meeting was now causing a number of complaints and had raised some apprehensions among members of the organization. The meeting featured a forum on the subject "Gay Christians and the Church," with several members of Lutherans Concerned invited as a panel to introduce the topic. Lutherans Concerned is an organization for gay and lesbian Lutherans as well as for nongays who share their concern for justice and understanding.[4] The person responsible for convincing the club's program committee to schedule this event was its chairperson, Bob Holmberg. One of Bob's sons was gay and had "come out" two years ago. After much agony, Bob and his wife, Arlene, had finally come to terms with their son's sexual orientation and had become avid readers of everything they could get their hands on concerning the subject. Bob was convinced the church needed to give serious attention to this matter and had called on several people he knew in Lutherans Concerned to participate in the program.

Some sixty persons came that night, a larger turnout than usual. Two gay persons, Steve and Carl, and a lesbian, Laurie, served as a panel. Bob made a few introductory remarks about the importance of the subject and then introduced the panel. All three gave a short account of their life stories with Steve speaking at greater length.

"I was raised," he began, "in a wonderful home with my brother and three sisters. My parents were fairly strict but not at all repressive. They were devout Christians, and much of our life centered about the church. I would have to say that my childhood was happy, with good memories of playing with a lot of kids in the neighborhood. I was around nine or ten when I really became aware that I was different from my buddies. It's hard to say what all I felt at that age, but I knew my feelings about sexuality were different. I made every attempt to relate to girls the way my friends did as I got into my high school years, but I couldn't. I became quite depressed whenever I would think about my 'secret,' and several times I thought of suicide. While in high school, I read a book published by my church's publishing house about sexuality. The author's point was that a gay person could change to straight if one had enough willpower and if one was given proper therapy. This gave me hope, and I decided to tell my parents how I felt and ask them if I could receive the therapy I needed.

"As I look back upon it now, it took a lot of courage for me to come out to my parents at that age. But I had confidence in them, and I wasn't disappointed. They were very understanding and hoped with me that therapy would help me to change. I spent a year with a psychiatrist who specialized in sexual problems, but it turned out to be a waste of time—I feel guilty to this day about the thousands of dollars my parents had to pay for that. There was a lot of conversation and some behavior modification techniques that left me feeling less than a human being. Finally I told my parents it was no use. I really don't think I could change my sexual orientation any more than any of you could change yours. During that time I was also dating a girl, but it was painful. I'm afraid she thought my lack of romantic interest was a reflection on her, but just the thought of making love to a woman was repugnant to me.

"During my sophomore year in college I started attending a gay and lesbian caucus, and through that organization I got acquainted with Tony. He and I have been living five years now in a relationship we expect to be permanent. During my college years I stopped going to church and generally felt alienated by the atmosphere I encountered there. Church members appeared to me to be the most opposed and narrow-minded about anything having to do with homosexuality. But then in my senior year at college I attended a forum on homosexuality and met the Lutheran student pastor, Rob Englehart. I got to talking to him afterwards, and that man's openness and compassion brought me into the Lutheran church. I'm now a member at St. Paul's on the other side of town, and just six weeks ago my pastor consecrated the home that Tony and I had moved into. It was a fantastic event for us and for our friends who were there from the congregation, both gays and straights. I guess something like that is the one liturgical event my church can provide for Tony and me to symbolize its support and bring a blessing to our relationship."

The question period that followed included moments of embarrassment and some expressions of hostility, but the openness and sincerity of the panel members established an atmosphere that put people at ease. One man wanted to know how the church could accept homosexual practice in view of what the Bible says about it. Another expressed concern about permissiveness in society and how it was creeping into the church. A woman was quite vehement in saying it was time the church led the way in changing its own attitudes and the attitudes of society toward gay people. "They have suffered long enough over the centuries," she said.

Bob Holmberg then brought the discussion to a close, concluding with a question that would not likely gain a unanimous answer from those in attendance: Where do we go from here?

In chapter 3, we noted the importance of knowledge to responsible moral judgments. One must be informed about the nature of the subject or situation that is being morally evaluated. This point is relevant to the reassessments now occurring among Christians concerning homosexuality.[5]

One area that has been extensively researched is the etiology of homosexuality, or its origin as a human sexual orientation.

Why a person is homosexually oriented is still not clear; scholars in this area do not agree. Through much of the twentieth century, the Freudian interpretation has held sway, maintaining that homosexuality is the result of an arrested psychosocial development due to a domineering mother and a distant father. In recent decades, more scholars are concluding that a number of reasons may account for the condition, including the possibility of a genetic predisposition. Whether of genetic or psychosocial origin (or a combination of both), it is clear that gays and lesbians *discover* their sexual preference rather than consciously willing to be homosexual. The investigations of Kinsey at the University of Indiana have established that human sexuality runs on a continuum from homosexual to heterosexual; everyone possesses both feminine and masculine traits, with the capacity to become oriented in either direction in terms of one's erotic preference. It appears that homosexuality is inherently part of the human condition, just as it is found among other animal species as well.

The social statements of churches concerning homosexuality reflect our expanding knowledge of the subject. Recent statements of a number of denominations now make a distinction between orientation and behavior, stating that one cannot be held morally accountable for one's orientation. However, most churches continue to reject homosexual behavior, or the practice of one's orientation. This conclusion reveals the continuing rejection of homosexuality, even if the individual is absolved of the condition he or she is in. Thus, abstinence is prescribed as the only acceptable life-style for homosexual people.

This judgment has been supported by what the church has understood the Scriptures to say about homosexuality. Very little in the Bible concerns the subject—three passages in the Old Testament and three in the New Testament are typically cited: Genesis 19; Lev. 18:22 and 20:13; Rom. 1:26-27; 1 Cor. 6:9; and 1 Tim. 1:10. Biblical scholars do not agree on the meaning of several of these passages (no Greek word can be translated to mean "homosexual" in the modern sense), nor is there consensus on the implications they bear for two persons like Steve and Tony. If the Romans passage is taken at face value beginning with verse 18, the presence of homosexual activity is itself an expression of divine wrath; because of the Gentiles' unwillingness to worship God and their resulting idolatry, God "gave them up to dishonorable passions" (Rom. 1:26). How can this passage be related to Christians who discover they are gay? Where is their unbelief that is being punished? Is it irrelevant to God and the Christian community whether they attempt to live responsibly with one partner, rather than promiscuously? Has God consigned them to a condition that does not allow them in good conscience to enjoy the intimacy that is a natural expression of that condition?

These are difficult and deeply frustrating questions for gay Christians. It would be much easier to ascribe their condition to a blind and arbitrary fate in a godless universe than to ascribe it to the God of Scripture. We know that "life is not fair," and people of faith and unbelief alike are often victims of mindless violence and tragic circumstances. However, while such victims inspire our concern and compassion, the homosexual person experiences intense hatred and rejection. What concerns should enter into a compassionate and discriminating evaluation of homosexuality?

Many Christians have modified their perspective on this topic, acknowledging that church and society in the past have been too harsh in their judgments. However, their desire to relate to the gay person in a spirit of Christian love is countered by the conviction that genital activity between people of the same sex is sinful. It usually involves not only the passages of Scripture already cited but an argument based on God's ordering of creation that intends all genital activity to be heterosexual. Homosexual expression is seen as a misuse of the human body, for it is contrary to God's design. Consequently, these Christians believe they are seeking the gay person's welfare before God and the human community by counseling sexual abstinence. Others would take a different approach, arguing for abstinence on the basis of possible consequences should church and society become more accepting of homosexual practice. If this were to occur, would not the next step be the legal recognition of homosexual relationships? Do we want equal recognition of heterosexual and so-called homosexual marriages? This concern is accompanied by the fear that a more open acceptance of the homosexual life-style will encourage those who are on the border to pass over into the gay world, increasing their number and exacerbating the tensions between the gay and straight communities.

Other Christians would take issue with the view that we can accept the homosexual orientation but condemn the behavior. They argue that in reality this is a rejection of the whole person, for the very being of gay people is denied if they are not allowed to act according to their sexual nature. Abstinence or celibacy is meaningful as a choice or witness of the individual, but to force it on gay people is to deny them as gay people. As far as Scripture is concerned, Christians who take this view are not convinced that Saint Paul is really addressing the situation we face today. The passage in Romans clearly assumes that it is heterosexuals who are engaging in homosexual activity as the result of a perverted and lustful desire ("the men likewise *gave up* natural relations with women . . ." [italics added]). Paul was not aware of what we today call inversion, or the fact that, for whatever reasons, certain people are constitutionally oriented toward the same sex in the expression of their erotic desire. Some suggest the apostle had in mind certain public spectacles, as when soldiers sodomized prisoners of war in public in order to humiliate the enemy. A recent author argues that Paul has in mind the practice of pederasty, erotic activity with boys.[6]

From this point of view, an appropriate alternative to prohibiting any kind of sexual activity among gays is to expect of them what we expect of the heterosexual community: to live in sexual intimacy with one other individual in a relationship of trust and fidelity. We call it marriage in the heterosexual world; it could best be called something else in the homosexual world. But whatever it is called, the possibility of gay couples establishing open and continuing relationships would help bring to the gay community a stability that until now has not been possible. Promiscuity and exploitation is encouraged by the kind of nether world in which gay people typically have been forced to live.

This subject provides a good example of the interplay between love and law in addressing a moral issue. Love toward one's homosexual neighbor seeks the neighbor's welfare. It is concerned that he or she be treated fairly and justly in a society that has been harsh and vindictive toward the homosexual person. It is concerned to see his or her humanity treated with the respect that is due any human being. This creates tension for many Christians because they also believe that homosexual activity is contrary to God's law. Law clearly serves the welfare of society by stating the limits for acceptable behavior; activity that transgresses the law is morally unacceptable and personally and socially destructive. What is the morally fitting resolution to this dilemma?

The Christian community will have to address the following questions in working out its response:

1. In view of the fact that gay people discover rather than choose their sexual orientation, and because one's sexuality is inherently a part of one's being and identity as a person, can the church in good conscience say to its gay members that the only religiously and morally acceptable life is one of sexual abstinence? Gay Christians understandably experience this restriction as a rejection of who they are—children of God whose orientation happens to be homosexual. Those who proclaim abstinence as the answer will often defend their position by referring to the restriction of abstinence placed upon alcoholics, whose alcoholism may be linked to a genetic predisposition. This analogy is inappropriate, however, because indulging or not indulging in alcoholic beverages is quite a different matter from expressing one's sexuality as a pervasive dimension of one's identity as a human being.

2. In the long run, is a more healthy sexual environment created by establishing social structures that expect and encourage responsible, "monogamous" relations between two homosexual persons? Is this a more just and humane expectation of gay people as well as one that would help to defuse the unhealthy homophobia that often prevails in the heterosexual community?

3. Pertinent to our attempt to arrive at a just and humane perspective on this issue is a further question: Is it possible to affirm the prevailing heterosexual orientation and at the same time to recognize the authenticity of the gay person's own sexual

identity? Can we recognize the normative character of hetero-sexual relationships and also recognize that the person who dis-covers he or she is homosexually oriented will expect, appropriately, to relate to others as a gay person? To force com-pliance with heterosexual practice becomes a traumatic assault on the being and integrity of gay people, forcing them to become someone they are not. We can be thankful for anyone's capacity to relate to another person as a sexual being so that one expe-riences a mutual, caring relationship in which maturation and growth can occur; this is God's gift to a person whether one's relationship to the other is within a homosexual or a heterosexual context. The challenge for Christians as well as for the larger society is to maintain an attitude of acceptance toward homo-sexual people and to expect them to conduct themselves re-sponsibly in their homosexual lives. At the same time, Christians should hold forth responsible heterosexual relationships as the model for the vast majority of the population.

As far as individual relationships are concerned, many Chris-tians remain embarrassed and ill at ease whenever they recognize the presence of gay people. It is a liberating experience to rec-ognize and affirm our common humanity with that of our neighbor who is gay, thus moving beyond the ignorance and stereotyping that burden heterosexual-homosexual relationships. We cannot do this, however, without affirming the integrity of the gay person *as* gay person. Once this is done, we can get beyond a person's sexual orientation and see that person as simply a human being like ourselves. We are all children of God; this is the reality that provides the beginning point for Christians. In our common humanity, we are loved by God, and we are called by God to live responsibly with each other. The Christian community must devote serious attention to all that this means in order to forge a just and responsible society as it relates to the gay person.

Should We Ever Choose Death?

The impact of technology in every area of social relationships has been profound, but it has been particularly dramatic in med-ical care. One focal point of this impact has been the care of the dying patient. Changes in this care resulting from the new technology have often forced difficult decisions upon families that gather around the deathbed of a loved one. The following incident illustrates a problem that has occurred with increasing frequency.

Glenn Roberson was fifty-seven and in good health. He often joked with his doctor that he wasn't giving her much business because he never seemed to need more than a couple of aspirins each year. This situation suddenly changed when Roberson suffered a gallstone attack that put him in the hospital. Surgery was required, and his doctor arranged with Dr. Everly, the general surgeon at the local hospital, to have the stone removed. Everly was also a friend of the family, having attended college with both Roberson and his late wife.

The operation was routine and seemed to be going well when suddenly Roberson had a cardiac arrest. The surgeon and anesthesiologist, using the defibrillator and several stimulants, worked frantically to get the heart going again, but it was between four and five minutes before they succeeded. The immediate question was whether there had been sufficient oxygen in the brain to avoid any impairment. Everly wanted to be optimistic, but he recognized that the chances of Roberson's surviving without serious brain damage were not very good. The problem at this point was that he could not tell just how serious the damage had been.

Roberson's wife had died from cancer less than two years earlier, leaving her husband and three children who were now in their twenties and thirties. As Dr. Everly spoke to the children and their aunt (Roberson's sister, who had been close to the family, particularly since the mother's death), he tried to describe the situation and to lay out the options as objectively as possible. He had been told by the sister early in their conversation that Roberson had expressed quite definitely his hope that he never be allowed to live "as a vegetable" should he end up in the intensive care unit.

"One never knows for sure," said Dr. Everly, "just how extensive the brain damage is in a case like this, but it could be quite bad. Only time will tell. We got him into ICU (intensive care unit) as quickly as possible, and more tests are being made. We'll do an electroencephalogram tomorrow—that's a test of his brain waves. We'll also see how he's responding by then. For now we can only wait."

Two days later it had become quite apparent that the damage was severe. Roberson was in a deep coma and hardly responded to intense pain. The neurologist reported severe brain disfunction; because the EEG showed some minimal activity, however, he could not be declared brain dead. Dr. Everly told the family that Roberson, attached to the respirator and being fed by a nasogastric tube, could linger on indefinitely—possibly weeks and months, even years. The daily costs for the care of Roberson in the ICU approached $1,500; insurance would cover the major portion of that amount, but coverage would not extend beyond one month.

During the first few days, the family was praying for a miracle. The pain of their mother's death was still lingering for the children, and they were hoping intensely that their father just might surprise them all by suddenly coming out of his coma. The one daughter was particularly adamant that prayer could change things, even when everything appeared to be hopeless. On the fifth day, the family and its pastor, together with Dr. Everly and the family doctor, gathered to discuss the situation.

"I'm afraid we're in exactly the situation that your father had hoped would never happen to him," said Dr. Everly. "What we're doing now is basically preventing your father from dying rather than nursing him back to health. The only reason for his continued breathing is the respirator that is doing it for him. Under these circumstances, it would not be inappropriate for you to decide to remove the respirator and let your father die."

The pastor and Roberson's sister supported this suggestion, with the pastor emphasizing that death had, in effect, already occurred because Roberson had been irrevocably removed from them. Now only machinery stood in the way of letting him depart. Though at first hesitant, the children were helped by this conversation to come to terms with the reality of their father's death. They decided to have the respirator removed and asked to be present when it was done in order to witness their father's final moments.

When the respirator was turned off, the breathing stopped and Roberson's complexion began to turn slightly blue. His heart rate dropped until, after several minutes, it finally reached forty beats per minute. Suddenly Roberson gasped and his heartbeat increased to fifty. A few moments later, he gasped again and then again. His heartbeat continued to rise and his breathing began to settle into a regular pattern. He was not going to die! Dr. Everly shook his head with a tight-lipped expression. He had not expected this and saw no reason for the expressions of joy that it elicited from the children. He suggested that they wait and see what happened during the next few days and then meet again.

At this next meeting, Dr. Everly confirmed what he had feared: the hopes of the family for a recovery were no more likely to be realized now than when Roberson was on a respirator. He could go on for years in this state, as in the case of Karen Ann Quinlan. The pastor asked if there were not similar cases in which the feeding tube was finally removed in order to let the patient die. Everly replied that some court cases recently had allowed for that to happen. "The feeding tube has been likened to the respirator in that both perform vital functions for the patient in order to maintain life."

The pastor spoke in favor of removing the nasogastric tube, for it was clearly unable to restore meaningful life to the children's father. The children expressed reservations about such an action because it appeared cruel to them to withdraw food, even if their father was comatose. The sister, who strongly resisted imposing this kind of "life" on her brother, made a more radical suggestion: "This may sound cruel, but I really believe we should feel an obligation to release Glenn from this horrible condition. Dr. Everly, can't you inject him with something that would end his life quickly and painlessly?"

Whether or not the sister's request is the most loving or morally fitting thing to do, Dr. Everly would be subject to the charge of murder if he were to follow her request. The Christian tradition has stressed human life as a gift from God, making us stewards rather than owners of our lives; we are not autonomous when it comes to choosing death over life. Mercy killing (euthanasia) has thus been condemned in this country, and love of neighbor has been interpreted as an imperative to do all that we can to maintain and restore the life of one who is sick and at the doorstep of death. The expression "sanctity of life" is often used to express and defend this position.

The new technology has changed the landscape for the care of the terminally ill and consequently has raised new issues for the ethics of terminal care. Glenn Roberson would have died on the surgeon's table in a previous generation. Now he is made a survivor but, unfortunately in his case, at the expense of meaningful life. For those caught in this kind of situation, the concept of euthanasia has had to be redefined. To *let* a person die by refraining from the use of artificial life supports, or to withdraw them in order to let a person die, is now defined as *passive* euthanasia. The traditional understanding of euthanasia as a direct action to hasten a person's death—by injecting an overdose of morphine, for example—is defined as *active* euthanasia. Protestant ethicists as well as churches that have addressed this issue have generally found passive euthanasia to be morally acceptable. This distinction has also been supported by the courts. It assumes that a critical threshold has been crossed by the patient and that death is now inevitable and the patient beyond reach (the fact that this is always a judgment call never makes the decision easy). Further treatment is now without purpose, and nothing more is done except to make the patient as comfortable as possible.

The fact that Roberson continues to breathe without the respirator confronts the family with a psychologically more difficult decision on whether to withdraw the feeding tube. Depriving a loved one of food, even if it is a colorless fluid being force-fed through a tube, is excruciatingly difficult. Nonetheless, the function of the feeding tube is analogous to that of the respirator in that both instruments serve to impose an activity necessary for life—eating and breathing—upon a person who is incapable of doing either. The facts of the matter must be reasonably clear, which in this situation involves an answer to whether sound medical advice allows for any reasonable chance of Roberson's recovery and of the possibility of relating to his family again. If such a development appears to be extremely remote, removing the feeding tube becomes a morally fitting action. Since meaningful life has now been denied to him, letting Roberson die by removing the support system becomes an act of love for him and for the suffering family.

Relating this situation to the teleological/deontological framework, some would argue that no human being should ever be an accomplice to the death of another human being, whatever the situation. The duty to preserve life is regarded as an absolute, which means that passive as well as active euthanasia ought to be rejected. "Thou shalt not cooperate in the death of a dying or hopelessly removed person" is a prohibition that allows for no exception. On the other hand, the teleological argument in this case might ascribe more value to Roberson's dying than to the life he was capable of "living." The pastor and sister of Roberson were defining life as more than a vegetative existence in which one's personal being is totally removed from everyone's reach. To live or to die under these circumstances was no longer a meaningful alternative, for Roberson was now caught in a "living death." To let him die was now a moral good that actually carried a moral obligation to allow it to happen.

What about active euthanasia? Can it ever be considered as a morally responsible act? One can understand why some would be driven to respond affirmatively to this question purely out of compassion for the dying person. But here we must draw a careful distinction. If the dying person (unlike Roberson) is still even remotely conscious, and thus still in relationship with us, we ought not intend the person's death and take action to execute that intention. Here is where the law serves as an appropriate limit to our sense of compassion. Taking the life of a person still in relationship with us, even a person experiencing intense pain, is to claim an autonomy over life that the Christian tradition has rightly rejected.

However, if a person has moved beyond consciousness and appears to be irreversibly beyond our reach, we face a moral situation that is qualitatively different. Under these circumstances, one might argue along with Roberson's sister that an overt act that terminates life would simply constitute a recognition that meaningful life is over. Nonetheless, as a rule, we should only take action that allows a person to die, rather than directly inflict death. In the case of a person near death who is suffering great pain, the legal prohibition of active euthanasia does not stand in the way of administering pain killers that ultimately hasten death. The care-giver is acting responsibly if the intention is to alleviate the pain and the actions taken are in harmony with that objective.

The moral dilemma we experience in a case like this results from our being pushed into the position of having to decide when a person is to die. We understandably shrink back from making that kind of decision, but modern technology will continue to present us with cases like Glenn Roberson's. What we are learning in these situations is that a rigid application of the historic Christian view of the sanctity of life may result in great burdens for the family and no meaningful gift of life to the patient. Indeed, to expend costly medical resources for a patient whose subsequent life is meaningless to him or her is itself an immoral act. When the prognosis allows for no reasonable hope of recovery, the patient is no longer capable of relating to others, and when dependence on heroic and costly life supports is essential to maintaining the signs of life, then removing those supports and letting the loved one die is the fitting choice. It is an act of love, based on the best medical advice available.

THE CHURCH IN SOCIETY

Making decisions is very much an individual matter. At the same time, Christians recognize that they are not alone in their moral responsibility. Who they are reflects the nurture and influence of the church, and who they are also contributes to the church's identity in the world. As an individual Christian, therefore, one is never an individual in contrast to the church but an individual who shares in the life of the church and who as a Christian bears both an individual and corporate identity and responsibility. In these two concluding chapters, we turn to the church as a decision-making body and raise the question, What is the responsibility of the church to society? As a religious and moral community, what are the perimeters of its witness?

The Imperative of a Social Witness

The church's first responsibility is to be clear about its mission. The church bears a message of good news for all people, the gospel of Jesus Christ. That message is *informative* in that it relates the story of Jesus who lived some 2,000 years ago and identifies him as God's Word in the midst of the human story. This message is not simply information, however. It is also *transformative*, for it is a message of God's love that inspires faith, hope, and love. The good news of divine grace creates new life in the repentant heart, and with new life comes new directions and goals. The whole person is engaged and opened to a life of discipleship; new priorities are forged in the conduct of one's life.

Not only the whole life of the believer, but the whole of life—every aspect of God's creation—is addressed by the Word of God. The church's message has a comprehensive character, placing the hearer in relationship to everyone else in the world and to the whole vast order of God's creation. In Saint Paul's cosmic vision, the whole creation is "groaning in travail," awaiting the transformation promised by the gospel (Rom. 8:18ff).

It has not been easy for most churches in the United States to capture this comprehensive vision. Much of American Protestantism, with its heritage of revivalism that emphasizes an intensely personal appropriation of the gospel, has tended until recently to limit its view of Christian responsibility to the life of the individual. This has been particularly true in the twentieth century following the failure of prohibition, after which conservative churches tended to concentrate on individual piety, stressing abstinence from a variety of personal and social vices. A strong code morality has been important in the personal upbringing and moral formation of Christians, but that upbringing has suffered from a spirit of legalism and a restricted view of Christian responsibility in the world.

The intense social upheavals of the 1960s compelled many Christians to challenge their churches to exert greater impact on society. It also stimulated theologians and ethicists in these churches to rediscover the social and global imperatives that are inherent to the church's message. Perhaps more today than ever before, Christians are willing to recognize that their accountability to God is a corporate as well as an individual matter. Their churches are more likely to acknowledge that their mission as communities of faith does not allow them to ignore the momentous moral issues that confront their own society and the world community. This is not to deny, however, that this subject poses serious problems for many Christians and continues to create divisions and antagonisms within the church.

Christians should recognize two important truths when they address this issue. First, individual and social morality are part of the same fabric of life. They cannot be separated in our thinking about morality without distorting our understanding of moral responsibility and compromising our effectiveness in responding to the moral challenges of our time. Second, the church has a witness to make in society *as church*, as a community of believers and not simply as individuals dispersed throughout society. The paragraphs that follow will elaborate each of these truths.

Considerable evidence suggests that personal morality and social morality are interdependent, each having an impact on the other. For example, a drug-ridden society is a broad social issue today that has an obvious impact on personal decisions concerning drug use. The more drugs are available and circulating, the more likely a person may choose to use them. To attack the issue at one level is obviously to attack it at the other. The international issue of arms control involves broad political and military policies. But in a society like ours, the actions that elected officials are willing to take on behalf of that goal will depend significantly on how many citizens are personally committed to it. Or again, standards of honesty in business and government as a whole carry an impact on personal decisions where one is challenged to deal honestly with a customer or client. Without belaboring the point, it is difficult to avoid the conclusion that all moral behavior bears both personal and social dimensions. This is a healthy recognition, particularly in a society that has made a sharp dichotomy between personal and public morality. Religion itself has been consigned to the personal, individual realm, compartmentalized and distorted by its removal from the momentous issues of public life.

One of the most important tasks of the church today is to resist this ideology that would privatize Christian belief and practice. When Christian faith becomes a purely private affair between myself and my God, truth becomes "my truth" and no one else's. If Christian ethics is understood as a purely personal and individual matter, it will have nothing to say beyond my own quest for ethical meaning and direction. We live in an age of relativism, which naturally thrives in a society that exalts the individual at the cost of community. It is important to emphasize that whether we speak in terms of God's love or God's law, the will and purpose of God as revealed in Scripture encompasses all of life, from the individual to the community, from personal to corporate life. The struggle for a just and humane life for every person in our society is not irrelevant or unimportant to the God of Scripture.

Suspicion of any kind of social involvement on the part of the church reflects an understanding of the human being that has prevailed since the Enlightenment. That understanding maintains the classical Greek division between a spiritual part of us, often called a soul, and our bodies or corporeal nature.[1] The assumption is that religious truth speaks to our spirit or soul with a message that pertains to the world to come. It is a message directing us to the life of the spirit, to the eternal, unchanging truths that transcend this life. For some Christians, this has literally entailed a physical withdrawal from the world. For Protestants, it has generally meant an intellectual and psychological division in our perception of the world, leading us to divide life into sacred and secular realms. This division has, in effect, restricted the message of the church to the "religious" realm and made it difficult to speak of the Christian's and the church's responsibility to society.

The second truth, that the church is called to address social issues as a community of faith, may not be as apparent to many Christians. It is hard to deny, however, that Christians who are engaged in witnessing to the centers of political and economic power both act with more influence and are more likely to be seen as a sign of God's presence in the world when they act corporately—as church—in affirming the cause of justice and condemning injustice. Individual witness in the social arena is necessary and obviously important, and the church is already involved through the Christian identity of such people. Yet this witness is dispersed and does not complete the responsibility of the church as an institution and community of faith. Acting intentionally as a community and standing together to make a witness in society is the clearest expression of the church's seriousness concerning its prophetic mission. It is an important dimension of the church's capacity to be a leaven in society.

Relating the point we are making to the reference in chapter 3 to law and gospel, we see a twofold witness of the church in society that reflects the Word of God as both law and gospel. This correlation can be expressed in the following diagram:

Word of God		Witness of the Church	
Law	Gospel	Prophetic Ministry	Evangelistic Ministry

While the distinction is crucial, the actual relating of law and gospel in personal experience and in the church's theology reflects the interaction of demand and promise and the impossibility of neatly dividing them according to a tidy formula. This diagram, therefore, does not do justice to the dialectic that goes on between law and gospel, but it does provide a framework by which to express the twofold nature of the church's witness.[2] While the gospel message can sensitize the Christian to the imperative to seek justice, it is the prophetic witness that proclaims God's sovereignty and calls those in positions of authority and power to be responsible before God in their exercise of that power.

Just as God's Word confronts the sinner in judgment, the church's witness should make plain to the powers that be that they are accountable to God and subject to God's judgment. Evangelism captures the "good news" mission of the church, but just as integral to its total witness is the church's prophetic ministry that confronts evil and supports the cause of justice. As the dominant center of political and economic power, the nation-state wields the most influence for both good and evil in the world and will necessarily draw the attention of the church's prophetic ministry. Decisions by those in elective office will often have profound consequences for the dignity of the individual person; the church cannot be oblivious to this reality. The church is not faithful to its mission if it chooses to ignore the misuse of power on the part of the powerful; its silence will function as a sanction of injustice.

It is critically important, then, to recognize that the mission of the church embodies its willingness to take a stand on behalf of what it perceives is right and just. In light of its message, the

church throughout history has ministered to those who are powerless and oppressed, fulfilling the role of "the good Samaritan"
who tends to the victim at the side of the road. Prophetic ministry
occurs with the recognition that the church's responsibility is not
limited to helping the victim at the side of the road. It must also
challenge those in authority to make the road more safe for its
travelers.

Ethicist Larry Rasmussen, in analyzing the public role of the
church, distinguishes three functions that it should fulfill: (1)
The church can be a community of moral deliberation on the
great public issues of the day; (2) the church can itself be a
community of moral formation; and (3) the church can be an
agent of moral action.[3] Each of these functions is important and
essential in its own right as well as being dependent upon each
other. The church as a community of moral deliberation has
often been a beam of light in totalitarian countries, claiming the
freedom to arrive at its own judgments in spite of its suppression.
As a community of moral formation that claims loyalty to an
exalted ideal of love, the church often functions as a seedbed
that nurtures the sensitive conscience and develops support for
those who work for a more just social order. That support will
be needed if the church itself is to be an agent of moral action.
To act is an expression of the church's integrity as a worshiping
and praying community as well as a moral community. The
church's faithfulness will express itself in taking concrete action
on behalf of those for whom it prays.

Addressing Social Issues: Problems and Conflicts

The tension within the Christian community over social
issues and the extent of the church's involvement with them was
noted in the experience of John and Blanche and Fred and Tina
in chapter 1. Their disagreements are found within every denomination, as well as between denominations. Some have a
tradition of fairly active engagement with social issues, while
many others have taken a more intentional approach during the
last several decades. This is generally true in regard to those
Protestant churches we often designate as mainline or old line,

such as the United Methodist, Episcopal, Lutheran, and Presbyterian churches. On the other hand, those churches that are characterized as evangelical and conservative, such as the Southern Baptist Convention, Pentecostal churches, and many smaller churches with Baptist or charismatic backgrounds, have traditionally been quite suspicious of any attempt on the part of churches to become engaged with social issues. That kind of activity has been branded as social gospel, in reference to the early twentieth-century movement to bring the church into the social struggle on behalf of the poor. This slogan has become an epithet for conservatives on both theological and political grounds. Theologically, social involvements of this kind are seen as an attempt to engineer salvation by bettering society rather than to trust in the God whose kingdom will come in its own good time. Politically, they are seen as capitulation to a politics of class warfare in which the church is guilty of partisanship by espousing the cause of the lower class.

Many have argued that the reason mainline churches are losing membership, or at best are doing little more than treading water, is due to their involvement with social issues. No doubt some people have left mainline denominations for this reason and in many instances have joined those churches or sectarian groups that restrict their message and activities to a gospel directed to the individual alone. A significant number do feel betrayed by the new spirit of social awareness, insisting that their church has been stolen from under them by leaders who have turned it into something other than what they have known.

A dramatic illustration of this reaction occurred a few years ago at the installation of the Right Reverend Edmond Lee Browning as presiding bishop of the Episcopal church. An old classmate of the bishop took the occasion to write an open letter in which he rehearsed the changes going on over the last several decades: the revision of the 1928 *Book of Common Prayer*, the ordination of women, and the spirit of social activism stemming from the 1960s. "Give us back our church," he wrote, "and you will be remembered as a good shepherd." This kind of lament needs sympathetic understanding and careful attention on the part of church leadership. The church does proclaim a message of peace and comfort to the individual, and many regard the church essentially as a haven from the tribulations of a fast-changing and often cruel world. But Christians who agree with the bishop's classmate need to examine their own motivations and whether their vision of the church allows it to be responsible to its mission. The task of bishops and pastors is to make clear the connection between the message of comfort and the message of challenge. Education within the church needs to dwell at length on the corporate responsibility of the people of God, whose loyalty to Jesus Christ will express itself in addressing the social ills that plague our communities and our nation.

If, in fact, the mainline churches are being marginalized at least in part because of their willingness to speak out on issues of justice and peace, this may actually be a blessing in disguise. It is comfortable to be part of the establishment, but the church's integrity is threatened whenever it becomes identified with it. The church can only be the church when it maintains a critical distance from the centers of power. If this results in the loss of members who themselves are too identified with structures of power and influence or who uncritically accept a prevailing national ideology, it hardly constitutes a mortal wound. It may even be the beginnings of a reformation in the church; in many instances, the finding of a social conscience rooted in God's Word has brought churches a sense of renewal and new joy in ministry. More than a few Christians have become more active in the church when they discovered that it was willing to be involved in addressing critical issues of our time.

We began this chapter with the statement that the church needs to be clear about its mission in the world. Our discussion to this point suggests that the church's mission is to proclaim the Word of God in all of its truth and power, both law and gospel, and to do so in a way that is sensitive to the historical, cultural, economic, and political setting in which the church is placed. The church's message is never proclaimed in a vacuum but in a particular time and place with particular life-and-death issues that concern the people who hear that message. Those life-and-death issues are always *moral* issues, involving individuals and groups of people in relation to other individuals and groups, raising questions of justice in the way political and economic power are exercised. It is not, finally, a matter of an individual gospel versus a social gospel but a recognition that the gospel reaches the individual in society who cries out for both love and justice. The love of God that promises salvation is not a promise that our yearnings for justice will be fulfilled, but we are assured that the God of the gospel is also the God who challenges the powerful and brings the imperative "to do justice, and to love kindness, and to walk humbly with your God" (Mic. 6:8).

Addressing Social Issues: Guidelines and Goals

Granted that the church as an institution and community has the responsibility to address issues of justice and peace, just how is that to be done? What kinds of decisions need to be made in order for the church to be a faithful and responsible witness in this realm of its ministry?

One temptation should be addressed before we go further. Just as it is inappropriate for the church to withdraw from the public realm and do nothing, it is also inappropriate for the church to claim a special authority for itself as though its ideas were always to be accepted as God's answers to the problems of society. The church and religious people generally are peculiarly vulnerable to this notion, which understandably is quite offensive to nonbelievers. It also reveals a misconception about the nature of what the church has to offer to the realm of public policy. It is helpful to note a parallel here to what we have said in regard to the impact of Christian faith on moral decision making at the individual level.

We have noted how Christian belief becomes a meaningful foundation for making moral decisions as it sensitizes people to the welfare of their neighbor. It gives the vision or ideal by which actions are guided. Prohibitions can get specific, for some forms of behavior are commonly recognized as destructive of other people and of personal relationships. But the positive imperative to love our neighbor, as we have seen, can go in many directions according to one's reading of the situation and the imagination and goodwill one brings to it. It is difficult to say that there is but one way of addressing a moral situation that challenges us to act constructively and positively on behalf of another.

The same applies to the church's responsibility to the political and economic establishment. It is relatively easy and obviously appropriate for the church to condemn instances of injustice in society, such as totalitarian acts of oppression or racist activities or economic policies that create an underclass of poverty whose hope for a better future is destroyed. When we consider what ought to be done to right these evil circumstances, we find much more room for disagreement. Given the complexities of political and economic life, people with the same goals will often differ over which policies the government should pursue in order to realize them. Consider the following experience of one particular church:

> The East Central Synod of a mainline denomination had been receiving petitions from congregations and pastoral groups concerning the increase of homeless people in the synod's principal urban center, Central City. The petitions expressed concern not only over the increasing numbers of homeless people but over the increasing incidence of whole families who were among the homeless. The petitions urged the synodical bishop, whose office was located in Central City, to bring the matter before the next synod assembly.
>
> Some petitions included proposals for action. One recommended that the synod promote a program involving congregations in Central City that would conduct a ministry to the homeless, with financial support coming from all the congregations in the synod. This included 150 congregations with a membership of 80,000, with some 40 congregations located in and around Central City. The proposal featured a cooperative program in which the parish units and other properties of several churches would be opened to families and others on a temporary basis, with employment assistance and referral services provided. A number of people would be employed on a part-time basis, with one full-time administrator who had considerable experience in a social service agency.
>
> The other proposals recommended that the church's concern be brought to city authorities and that the government take greater initiative in attempting to solve the problem. At the synod assembly, after considerable debate, it was decided that the bishop and a group of pastors should meet with the mayor and members of the city

council, urging legislation that would enable the city to launch a meaningful program of assistance to the homeless. The meeting was successful in highlighting the seriousness of the problem and the moral obligation of the city's leadership to galvanize public support. The bishop and pastors promised to do what they could to sensitize their people concerning the seriousness of the problem.

Within a few months, the city council was considering the merits of two proposals. One was a modified revival of a bill, defeated two years earlier, that would commit the city to a public housing project providing one hundred apartments in several buildings to be erected near the downtown area. Rent would be subsidized and the eligibility of residents would be based on need. Discussion of this proposal centered on whether the city could afford it, whether it was too ambitious for the actual needs of the homeless, and whether the city's taxpayers would be willing to support it.

The second proposal would clearly be much more modest in its impact, involving thirty to thirty-five apartments through the renovation of vacant and deteriorating properties at several points in the city. This option featured an innovative arrangement between the city and private industry, with the latter encouraged to become involved in the project through financial incentives. It would involve less expense to the taxpayer, but its impact would also be less. Discussion of this option revealed a fair amount of concern over whether it was a sufficient response to the problem the city was facing.

The synod council, a group of twenty-one pastors and laity that conducted the synod's affairs between the annual gathering of the assembly, was meeting just when the housing proposals were being debated in city hall. There was general satisfaction that finally something was getting done, but a number of pastors and lay people were quite upset that the more modest proposal was being seriously considered. They urged the council to issue a statement in support of the more ambitious plan, arguing that even one hundred new dwellings would not begin to solve the problem. Others felt strongly that the cost of that proposal made it prohibitive; they argued the merits of realism and that a modest beginning was at least better than nothing.

What should the council do?

The East Central Synod is facing a common problem arising whenever the church addresses social issues: What are the proper boundaries of the church's involvement in public policy decisions? Some would say the church should restrict itself to its own activities—the good Samaritan role—and do no more than what the one proposal advocated, with church dollars supporting a program of assistance and referral services. This ignores the capacity of the church to exert influence as a community of faith upon those who are responsible for the welfare of the citizenry. Those who wield political power are obligated to use it responsibly on behalf of all citizens, and their capacity for achieving responsible goals far exceeds what the church can do with its limited resources. The church should do what it can through the voluntary support of its members, but government is also obligated to be responsive to the moral concerns of the people.

Some would question whether the bishop and others should ever sit down with political leadership and, in effect, lobby for political action. On the other hand, here is an instance of clear human need involving personal tragedy for a significant number of people. While it is not advisable for churches to try to influence public servants on this scale on a regular basis, critical situations can lead to appropriate efforts of this kind. Note that the church is not acting on behalf of itself as an institution in society but on behalf of people who are in difficulty and who have virtually no power to do anything about their situation.

No simple answer resolves the problem of appropriate boundaries to the church's activity in the realm of public policy. A general principle, however, is that the church has something important to say when the question is, What is our moral obligation in this situation? Once that question is answered, we move on to ask, How shall we best carry out that obligation? As we move from a moral question to this next question involving strategy, the church should recognize that it does not deliver a Word of the Lord at this level of decision making (which is not to deny that figuring out strategy can also involve some moral issues). The complexities of hammering out legislation will involve the balancing of political realities and the fine art of compromise. Here the most we can expect is that the people's representatives act honestly on behalf of the public interest as they see it. In the above case, any further involvement of the synod council would result in possibly bitter division for no justifiable reason. Individuals may well want to express their views to members of the city council, but as individuals rather than representatives of the church.

A principal role of the church in addressing social issues is that of teacher, both to its own membership and to all whose attention can be reached. It can exercise a long-range impact by educating its members concerning the moral implications of social issues, enabling Christians to gain a better grasp of the dimensions of an issue and consequently to come to a more responsible judgment. This means that churches must utilize many resources in addressing an issue, bringing together experts from the social sciences and humanities, ethics, and theology. People who are directly affected by the issue should also be included, as well as others who are not "experts" but whose life experience enables them to contribute wisdom and commonsense knowledge. A church's Office of Church and Society can make a significant contribution by gathering such people and publishing the results of their work, providing continuing analyses of a variety of issues. Several features should characterize these efforts: careful attention to the empirical dimensions of the issue (the "facts of the matter") that are indispensable to sound moral judgment; clarification of the theological convictions that underlie the stance taken; and an objective spirit that cuts through partisan positions and exposes the fundamental moral issues at stake. In their preparation, these statements should come under the review of a significant number of the church's congregations so that the wisdom of the people is heard and a sense of ownership has been developed prior to the church's adoption of a social statement.

While the church's vision of a just society will sensitize it to the plight of those who are victimized and powerless to change their condition, in many issues it is unclear who is the victim of injustice. Indeed, the greater the ambiguity, the more intense the issue becomes, particularly where matters of life and death are involved. Abortion and capital punishment are two examples in contemporary society where people are having difficulty determining the moral status of both the fetus and the criminal in view of arguments that justify destroying them on explicitly moral grounds.

"Issues" in society are always characterized by conflicting values that we have difficulty balancing. The more bewildering this conflict, the more appropriate it is for the church itself to withhold judgment. Here the church's teaching function is particularly important, analyzing the grounds by which people arrive at differing viewpoints and assisting church members to arrive at a responsible, informed position. Churches must also realize that not every issue emerging on the horizon of public interest warrants the consideration of the church. Questions like the following are appropriate to raise: Is this an issue that poses serious religious and ethical questions for many people? Does it involve injustice that is life-threatening to people or that constitutes a serious assault on their personal welfare? Is it an issue on which the church can possibly exert significant impact?

Churches risk being politicized when they take seriously their responsibility to join in the struggle for justice and a more humane world. While that risk does not justify the church's forsaking the struggle, it does require continual self-examination to make sure that its response is theologically and morally inspired rather than dictated by a particular ideology (a subject to which we will give more attention in the next chapter). The reasons for taking a stance must be rigorously examined, and the boundaries of the church's capacity to deliver judgments should be carefully reviewed. However responsible a church may be in the stands it takes, some will always suspect its motives or accuse it of assuming a partisan position. In both the style and the substance of its stands, the church's concern must be evident to clarify the theological and ethical dimensions of the issue being addressed and to demonstrate by this effort that the church is not owned by any particular interest or group.

Whenever we address the subject of the church in society, we must remember that we are not talking about saving a sinful world by seeking to make it more just. It is not a matter of salvation or the justification of sinners when we talk about personal or social ethics. We are addressing the *response* of the church to the Word of God, both law and gospel, in which we recognize our responsibility as justified sinners to work for justice and peace. God alone justifies because God alone has the Word and the creative authority to do that. Our task lies in our response to that Word on both the individual and corporate level, joining with all people of goodwill to struggle for a more just and humane world. The language of both justification and justice are part of the church's witness to God's presence in the world, but the distinction is crucial. We witness and work in both realms, but stress the overriding importance of recognizing the divine mystery and sovereignty in the one and our human responsibility in the other.

The Witness of the Congregation

To be a part of the church for the individual Christian is to be a member of a congregation, an often small group of Christians—most likely fifty to three hundred or four hundred men, women, and children—who gather on Sunday mornings to worship. In addition to being a worshiping community, the congregation is also a learning community, engaged in a program of Christian education stretching from preschool-aged children to adults. As communities of faith, congregations are also moral communities that are called to obedience by the Lord of the church. To this point, our reference to corporate responsibility has meant the church in its nationwide or synodical form, consisting of many congregations. Now we focus on the fundamental level of the congregation itself and inquire what it means for St. Paul Lutheran Church in Centerville or Trinity Methodist Church in Middleburg to be obedient to their mission. Our inquiry assumes that there is such a thing as congregational responsibility and that each congregation is obligated to ask itself, What are we called to be and to do in this place?

A congregation's social witness needs careful consideration. The reflection and planning that go into this matter will obviously be influenced by the individuals who assume a leadership role. They must recognize the importance of generating wide support in the congregation. Any appearance of an elitist group that constitutes a well-defined minority in pushing social concerns should be avoided, even though this is not always easy. This is where education and leadership are crucial. The importance of the congregation's witness needs to be established through classes at all levels of the youth and adult education program. Speakers and special events planned for meetings of organizations within the congregation can also be helpful in highlighting issues and encouraging greater social awareness as a community of faith. It is a long-term project, demanding patience and persistence and the involvement of people important to the life of the congregation.

The location of the congregation will have a bearing on the shape of its social ministry. A rural setting will automatically raise issues in agriculture, such as rural poverty, the small farmer, and agricultural trade policies. The immediate issues confronted by an inner-city parish will be quite different. At the same time, the vision of each congregation should be broader than the immediate issues of its own community. Addressing social issues should help us recognize the interdependence of a technological society and the responsibilities shared by everyone on behalf of the common good.

Whatever the congregation's geographical setting, certain areas of human need are bound to be common in one form or another to all localities and may offer particular opportunities for service. One congregation in Ithaca, New York, defined four areas that invited its attention: (1) food, clothing, and shelter; (2) the young and the elderly; (3) the handicapped; and (4) the desperate. [4]

What the congregation can do in each of these areas depends on the kind of needs it encounters, the scope of those needs, the presence of governmental or voluntary agencies that are addressing them, and the financial and human resources of the congregation. Where professional assistance is needed, the congregation can serve as a referral resource, directing people to institutions or agencies where help is available. Larger congregations can develop their own programs of supportive services, or congregations can pool their efforts in maintaining food banks and soup kitchens, tutorial and literacy programs, counseling services, and the like. Whatever the program or activity, it must involve careful assessment of the need and the available resources to meet that need.

As a moral and learning community, the congregation fulfills its calling both by reaching out to others in concrete activity and by forming and informing itself through a program of learning. This is where the educational program of the congregation is critical, informing and sensitizing its members to local, national, and global issues. Too many congregations totally ignore the area of Christian ethics and contemporary moral issues in their educational programs. The reasons for this are several, and they often overlap: it may reflect a denominational heritage that lacks a strong tradition of social action; the congregation may believe it lacks the leadership and the interest needed to generate a lively forum on social issues; or those responsible may be fearful about possible embarrassment and divisiveness that a consideration of social issues might cause. While these reasons can pose formidable obstacles, none of them can justify the silence and inactivity in any number of congregations.

It is important for the congregation's educational program to include social issues because learning is essential to the quality of the congregation's witness and the individual Christian's witness. Of course, this depends, in turn, on the quality of the learning that goes on in the congregation. Teachers and those in charge of the educational program must seek to transcend the ideological differences that so easily polarize people and get in the way of genuine education. Whether the issue is abortion, euthanasia, a local labor dispute, a school bond issue, or nuclear weapons, the challenge is to clarify the moral issues at stake. Since these issues are invariably marked by values placed in opposition to each other, the task of a learning group is to carefully balance these values and come to what appears to be the most responsible conclusion. This may or may not result in a consensus of the group, but participants should be challenged to understand just why and how they arrive at the judgments they make. Oftentimes the materials issued by the congregation's denomination can serve quite well in focusing the discussion.

Because moral issues are often emotion laden, people will feel strongly about their views and even respond with indignation toward a person who disagrees with them. Christians are also tempted to assume that their position on a moral issue reflects the very mind of God, which accounts for the greater indignation often found among Christians who run into disagreements! Our earlier discussion (chapter 2) on the appropriate use of Scripture for moral decision making should make clear the mistake involved in such an assumption. People on either side of every profound moral issue in our society can usually stand on solid ground, and the Word of God is not likely to issue a clear and definitive answer to any issue on which Christians find themselves in continuing and fundamental disagreement.

The answer to this reality is not to give up on addressing these issues as a Christian community, for genuine disagreement can lead to much learning and growth. One of my most rewarding experiences while conducting a Sunday morning class on social issues was the direct result of the fact that the participants represented such a wide variety of ideological positions. One was an elderly lady, an intense social activist and chairperson of the local chapter of Americans for Democratic Action (often characterized as the liberal wing of the Democratic Party). Several in the class shared many of her views. On the other side were those who felt at home in the conservative wing of the Republican Party, expressing staunch support of President Reagan's policies. With these two poles strongly represented, the discussion at times became more than lively, bordering on resentful opposition. Yet, the joy of this experience was the willingness of each side to recognize the other as brothers and sisters in Christ, to listen to and learn from each other, and to recognize that no one could claim to speak for God or for the church. The church—and the local congregation in particular—should be the home for people of all political and economic persuasions, from libertarians to socialists, recognizing that even the most strongly felt differences cannot destroy the bond of our common loyalty to Jesus Christ.

The authority of the clergy in most churches gives them significant responsibility for the effectiveness of a social ministry program. This does not mean that pastors should take leadership roles, necessarily, but they need to be visible in helping to facilitate the program. In their teaching and preaching, they have ample opportunity to develop the awareness of their congregations to issues of social justice. These issues are best addressed in the classroom or public forum, where people on all sides of an issue can freely express themselves and Christian concerns can be raised in an atmosphere of give-and-take. The pastor ought not pose as an expert on any particular social issue any more than other members of the congregation who have made themselves well informed through serious study and exposure to the issue.

As a rule, references to social issues in the pulpit are best made to illustrate or make a point in regard to the text on which the sermon is based, rather than using the pulpit to address head-on a particular issue. An exception to this rule would depend on the seriousness of the issue and the extent of its infringement upon the life and experience of the congregation. What the pastor says should not be marked by partisanship but should help the congregation clarify its perception of the issue and should suggest some possible implications from the Christian message and tradition that have bearing on it. From a pastor's preaching through the years, the congregation should be able to sense a concern for justice and the conviction that the church does have a message to bring to the powers and principalities of our time. On the other hand, pastors seriously compromise their witness when they become so absorbed with social issues that their ministry is largely defined by them. Whenever a pulpit is turned into a soapbox, the pastor's ministry loses credibility and the life of the congregation can be seriously threatened.

Our conclusion, then, is that the church at its various levels of organization bears an imperative to witness to society on behalf of the common good and that imperative is rooted in God's Word as both law and gospel. The moral life of individuals and the moral life of society mesh together so that individual and social morality are inseparable. The church's responsibility to individual Christians and their desire to live faithfully as followers of Christ thus brings the church face-to-face with the moral challenges of society. It is called to respond with deeds of love, with words of challenge and judgment, with moral teaching and nurture, and with holding forth a vision of community in which justice shall reign.

6 CHRISTIANS ON THE LEFT AND RIGHT

The involvement of the church in society on behalf of concerns relating to justice and peace raises some serious theological and political issues, as we have seen. What complicates the picture further is the fact that political and economic issues are often dominated by ideological positions. Ideology is not easy to define because it is a term used in many different contexts. Generally, we can say that an ideology conveys a vision of what society ought to be, involving what one believes to be an appropriate ordering of economic and political life. In the context of the world struggle between East and West that has dominated the decades since World War II, one can speak of Marxism (now in retreat) and liberalism (the Western tradition) as the two major ideological forces. At the moment, we want to focus more narrowly on the ideological conflict within our own society, usually expressed in the terms *liberalism* vs. *conservatism*. This might be termed a family dispute within the Western tradition, involving many common assumptions but also opposing economic and political viewpoints on what needs to be done in order to arrive at the kind of society in which we want to live.

There has been a growing tendency to see every public issue in terms of a conservative or liberal perspective. This means that particular points of view are more likely to be assessed on the basis of how they fit in an ideological mind-set rather than to attempt to honestly evaluate their moral, political, and economic merits. People who are normally capable of being objective and dispassionate can become quite emotional and biased when the discussion of an issue challenges the validity of their ideological position. The temperature level is also boosted if the stand taken by one's church on a particular social issue is perceived to be in opposition to one's own ideological stance. Because of the impact of ideology on our approach to social issues, we need to consider how it relates to the church's involvement in society.

The Impact of Ideology

The following conversation illustrates a conflict that has been more apparent in recent years as churches have become more intentional about addressing issues of public policy.

> St. James Lutheran Church is located in an upper-middle-class sec-
> tion of the state's capital city. Its membership includes a fairly high
> percentage of college-educated people and leaders in the business
> and professional worlds. The state university as well as several private
> colleges and technical schools add to the attractiveness of the com-
> munity, placing education as well as government among the city's
> principal employers. Each fall and spring a particular feature of the
> adult education program at St. James is a class conducted by Pastor
> Moore that runs for eight weeks and involves a covenant on the
> part of the participants to read the class materials in preparation for
> each session. The current class has been studying four social state-
> ments adopted by the congregation's national church body, including
> one on the economic order.
> An intensely interested and vocal participant in the class has been
> Robert Lake, a vice president at one of the local banks. During one
> session, Lake expressed considerable discontent with the church's
> statement on the economic order. It was, he said, "too socialist a
> document" to be acceptable. Pastor Moore asked him if he could
> elaborate on what he meant by "socialist."
> "I mean," said Lake, "that there is a bias in this statement toward
> equality at the expense of freedom. It stresses economic justice, and
> I have no problem with that, but it doesn't recognize that the engine
> for any successful economic system is individual and corporate self-
> interest. It's a cruel world out there, and some are going to get more
> and some are going to get less because we aren't equal. Equality is

a myth; the only way you can get economic equality is to make a 'Big Brother' out of the government, which is what the Communists are doing. They kill their economy when they try to make everyone equal."

At this point another participant, Donna Rowe, entered the conversation. Rowe was a biology professor at one of the local colleges who had gained a high profile in recent years as a leader in a statewide organization advocating environmental responsibility. "My impression, Robert," she began, "is just the opposite. This statement is obviously leaning over backwards to avoid any hint that it is *not* procapitalist. It's difficult for any church in this country to advocate significant change in our economic system, regardless of how unjust that system might be. I personally think that something is fundamentally wrong with any economy that creates a little minority of millionaires and even a few billionaires who control it and a large number of poverty-stricken, unemployed people. That's our situation right now, and I'm convinced we are in deep trouble."

Lake was not convinced. "My point is that we must not let our liberal ideals control and ultimately kill our capitalistic system," he said, moving to the edge of his seat. "We are in danger of killing the goose that lays the golden egg. The more freedom we give 'big business'—and that's not a negative term—the more wealth we create, and the more there is to spread around. The poor in this country are still better off than the poor in most other countries."

"But certainly you recognize," returned Rowe, "that we have created a large underclass of people who have no hope of sharing in the so-called American dream. Economic freedom is no absolute; it must be controlled by our ideals of social justice that would guarantee a share for everyone in the economic pie. I realize that some people will always make more than other people, but our society is threatened whenever the difference becomes as great as it is now. I think our whole system borders on obscenity."

"Your morality is getting out of control," laughed Lake. "Seriously, the only way our economy will serve the greatest number is if we give it the freedom to operate within the controls of the marketplace. A minimum of regulation is needed, but I firmly believe that our system is self-correcting if it is basically left alone. You must also recognize, Donna, that legislating ideals of equality is always a tricky business. My sense of equality is not yours, and no one, least of all the government, should think it can create a master plan in which perfect justice can be attained. I should think our church would recognize that fact and emphasize it in this kind of statement."

This brief exchange reveals several characteristics of conservative and liberal thinking as they relate to economics. Conservatives are confident of capitalism, maintaining (at least theoretically) the desirability of the least amount of governmental interference as possible. They make economic freedom the foundation stone for all other freedoms prized by our democratic heritage. Government is the principal threat to that freedom, whether it acts for ostensibly just and admirable reasons or for other reasons. The entrepreneur is the classic American model, embodying what is great and durable about this country; the competition of the free market stimulates entrepreneurship and the productivity of the economy, which works to the benefit of everyone, rich and poor.

Conservatives are skeptical about attaining a just society on any comprehensive scale. They are dubious about our capacity to engineer social change, for to do so both assumes more control than we actually have and ignores the assault on individual freedoms that results from control "from the top down." Conservatives who are moved by a social conscience are more apt to find fulfillment in efforts of smaller, voluntary groups with more limited objectives. They believe that people who collaborate on the local scene to achieve a good objective are more likely to exercise a direct impact and accomplish a concrete good. Social activists are seen as naive "do-gooders" who often, if not invariably, are moved by their own needs rather than by a realistic assessment of a social issue.

Liberals are more confident of the government's capacity to create conditions that contribute to social welfare and are less confident that a free economy will work to the maximum benefit of all the people. They are generally committed to capitalism but are convinced of the necessity of strict government monitoring in order to curb its excesses. They believe that the federal governments, with its resources and its power to maintain uniform standards, should ultimately be responsible for maintaining the social welfare "net" that would prevent people from being victimized by chronic poverty.

These orientations toward economics and politics that we call conservatism and liberalism possess implications that reach into many dimensions of life, taking on the character of a world-view. Liberals are characterized as open to change and innovation; conservatives are intent on conserving wisdom from the past. Liberals are likely to be pragmatic, searching for new expressions of value; conservatives stress continuing values and universal norms. Liberals are likely to be critical of nationalist aspirations and expressions of United States military power; conservatives take pride in the power and international stature of their country. Liberals are inclined to recognize the idealism in Marxist thought and to push for dialogue rather than categorical condemnation of communism; conservatives generally see Marxism and communism as irredeemable and intent on destroying the West.

Because of the far-reaching extent of one's liberal or conservative orientation and because these orientations are value-laden and thus bear considerable emotional and personal weight, they tend to become primary categories for identifying people. We often regard the conservative or liberal label as the most significant knowledge we can gain concerning another person; the ideological label serves, unfortunately, as a means of categorizing and even stereotyping a person's beliefs and life-style. This stereotyping may occur in our attitudes toward ourselves, where we gain a certain satisfaction in identifying ourselves with other people who share the same fundamental outlooks on life. We feel comfortable with such people and easily assume a "we-they" attitude that accentuates the differences between our group and those in the opposing ideological camp.

The term *ideology* expresses this character of we vs. they. It usually refers to beliefs that both express our personal convictions and provide an identity for our group. This group consciousness brings its impact upon our convictions so that they serve the interests of the group as it defines itself in opposition to other ideological groups. Thus, self-interest and group bias become a part of ideology, heightening the differences and tensions between people. Robert Lake, for example, was not only expressing a conservative economic philosophy but also a view that expresses the interests of those who are engaged as leaders in the world of business. As a banker, his own thinking naturally tends to reflect the interests and goals of his associates in the business world.

Donna Rowe, as a biologist in the quite different world of aca-
demia, is not in a position that is likely to encourage an appreciation of Lake's concerns. As an environmentalist who is
sensitive to the excesses of the industrial world, she tends to look
suspiciously at arguments on behalf of business.

We should not leave the impression that everyone falls into
either the conservative or liberal camp. These terms are in fact
nebulous enough to make one question their usefulness; any
definition is bound to appear arbitrary or inaccurate to many.
The divergence among people who would regard themselves as
liberal or conservative makes these terms particularly problematic
when applied like labels to individuals. In spite of this lamentable
fact, these terms will persist as long as they continue to identify
those ideas and attitudes we have been discussing. What is hap-
pening more frequently as these terms are increasingly used as
epithets to label the "other side" is the use of modifiers that
emphasize the extremism of the opposition's ideology. People in
the other camp are called *ultra*-liberal or *ultra*-conservative or
radical liberal or *reactionary* conservative. This kind of termi-
nology is used to discredit the opponent by suggesting that he
or she is far removed from the mainstream of society. It also
reflects the fact that, for the person in one camp, anyone in the
other is bound to appear far removed from responsible attitudes
and thinking.

Nor should our use of these terms suggest that people who
fall into a liberal or conservative way of thinking are consequently
dominated by a kind of party line that prohibits independent
thought. The extent to which this may be true depends on one's
relation to the group that informs one's thinking. Many people
are content to let others do their thinking for them, and knowing
the party line is both a source of personal satisfaction and a
confirmation of one's identity. All of us, of course, tend to respond
to those journals, newspapers, commentators, and associations
that confirm us in our ideological persuasions. Both personally
and socially, the pressures to stay on our ideological course can
be very strong indeed. To move away from it will likely result in
a move to a "new world" with new friends and new resources for
informing oneself and understanding one's world. However, the

capacity to maintain one's independence and to cultivate a frame of mind that is open to opposing perspectives remains an option for everyone, though this capacity will vary from one person to another.

Ideology and the Church

It is also the character of ideology to assume the dimensions of religion. If we define religion as convictions by which one defines reality and one's own role within it, then ideology can function as a religion. This is most obvious where ideology assumes totalitarian form as in fascism and communism. Here we have explicit attempts to claim transcendent meaning and value on behalf of the state or the party and even on behalf of specific human beings (*Der Fuehrer*). The expression of ideology in conservatism and liberalism within the context of Western democracy does not involve transcendent claims, nor does it make claims for a total loyalty and commitment like that demanded by a state or by an authoritarian party. Nonetheless, for any number of people a conservative or liberal philosophy of life is the constellation of ideas that defines their lives in relation to their world. When these philosophies take on an ideological character in which one identifies one's outlook with the interests of one's group, the potential for conflict is obviously increased. This has implications for the church in its involvement with social issues and for Christians who often share the ideological stance of a particular group.

When the church addresses social issues it naturally makes itself vulnerable to charges of ideological influence. Mainline churches are commonly accused of liberalism, and evangelical and fundamentalist churches are branded conservative. We noted in the previous chapter the importance of objectivity and balance on the part of church leadership in addressing issues of public policy. This imperative is heightened in view of the tendency to read every response in terms of an ideological loyalty. One proper concern of the church is to encourage society to seek a middle ground between opposing views, challenging each side to recognize the validity in the concerns of the other. Given the fact that a social issue usually emerges because of legitimate values being placed in competition with each other, the challenge is always to bring a sympathetic hearing to each of these competing values and possibly to reach an acceptable middle ground.[1] The particular disservice that ideologists impose on public debate is the refusal to listen to their opponents; the church must not hesitate to challenge this attitude, for it not only undermines the assumptions on which a free society is based but impugns the worth and integrity of the opposition.

While the church may make its contribution in establishing a middle ground and effecting some degree of reconciliation, some issues cannot be resolved in this way. The primary concern of the church in the public realm should be to establish justice, encouraging a society that is eminently fair in its treatment of all citizens and that stimulates a commitment on the part of everyone to the common good. In an increasingly heterogeneous society, this is a most demanding task, and the church must pursue all the more aggressively its function as a goad that pricks the conscience of society to make it sensitive to injustice wherever it is found. This must be done regardless of whom it offends. Of course, differing ideological perspectives will give a variety of answers about what constitutes justice and what measures are called for on the part of government to effect it. Nonetheless, the church has an imperative to dramatize the plight of those who are victims of society—the poverty-stricken, the vulnerable—in an effort to transcend ideological differences and appeal to the humanity and conscience of society. Where the need is obvious and clearly perceived, ideological differences will more likely be transcended and a consensus developed that leads to action.

In its responsibility to avoid being ideologically imprisoned, the church's faith serves a self-critical function that should keep it honest concerning its motives and the ethical stance it assumes in addressing social issues. In this context, the church's faith is most immediately the faith of those in leadership positions who are responsible to develop and define the church's stance on these issues. Every stance taken by the church requires self-examination and the admission that the church has no claim to infallibility as it seeks to be faithful in the public realm. We cannot claim for ourselves the fullness of knowledge that belongs to God alone. Christian faith recognizes our sinfulness, which here is best understood as our pride that moves us to claim perfection for ourselves and our causes. Faith in God revealed in Jesus Christ is a faith that impels us to practice self-criticism, recognizing that ideological pretensions are but one attempt among many to forge some sense of security for ourselves. If we fail to hear the fullness of the gospel message, even our knowledge of Jesus Christ can be turned into a rod of self-righteousness with which to beat our opponents.

It is important to recognize that what we mean by a self-critical spirit is much more than an intellectual stance. It is, rather, the expression of our whole existence in which we recognize, in a spirit of repentance, our human fallibility and our endless potential to manipulate the truth so that it fits our desires. The self-critical spirit will enable us to challenge our tendency to read the empirical data with a bias that validates those conclusions and those values most important to us. The spirit of self-criticism is necessary in order to keep us honest before God and our fellow human beings.

The English historian and Christian Herbert Butterfield has been particularly astute in identifying the spirit of self-righteousness as the critical moral issue in international relations.[2] He notes that the principal moral challenge is to exercise self-judgment, a challenge that is compounded when one moves from the individual level to that of the group. The struggle between East and West has swept not only individuals but nations into ideological conflict, and nations are least open to the spirit of self-examination and self-criticism required to overcome self-righteousness. Without this moral self-judgment, the possibility of meaningful dialogue based on a willingness to listen and to hear the opposition is hardly possible. The church should be a leaven that encourages this kind of honesty in the public realm.

Finally, the church must challenge the bitter polarization that always occurs in ideological conflict. Such conflict distorts the critical issues of our time by creating its own particular, warped context for their discussion and possible action. The church in this situation should not be afraid to confront those powers that seek to intensify conflict and limit the possibilities for understanding and reconciliation. As a prophetic community, the church should be providing a counterpoint to the message and deeds of the establishment, particularly when it is moved by an exaggerated self-interest and needs to be challenged.

Christians on the Left

In recent years, liberalism has come upon hard times in American society. As the dreaded "L" word, it has become associated with fiscal irresponsibility, a naive "bleeding heart" approach to society's underclass, permissiveness in regard to personal morality that has eroded standards of conduct, and lack of confidence in the United States in the ideological struggle with the Communist world. The traditional values of liberalism that have led to a concern for those on the bottom rungs of the economic ladder have been questioned and disparaged as the ideological temper of the country has taken a pendulum swing to the right.

Nonetheless, many Christians have found a liberal stance appealing precisely because it has stood up for the less privileged and the vulnerable segments of our society. Liberally oriented people have been the ones concerned about the rights of racial minorities, women, and those living in poverty. Issues of social justice are usually pursued and supported by those who would consider themselves as political liberals, even though this term covers a variety of perspectives on specific issues.

Historically, the liberal stance has embodied an understanding of human nature that is basically optimistic, holding forth the prospect of human progress and confident that an enlightened government and educated people can achieve a just and fair society. The greatest challenge to any society, it has maintained, is to overcome the limitations imposed by ignorance and to let the light of reason show the way to a better world. Christians (particularly those shaped by the Reformation tradition) do not share this confidence in reason, recognizing that our self-centeredness can control and direct our rational life in ways that are destructive of human community. Therefore, Christians of a liberal persuasion will not be as confident in the ability of government to steer the way to a better society. They do believe, however, that meaningful progress can be made toward a more just society if the government is seriously intent on being the representative of *all* the people and is directed by a sensitive social conscience, goals that are worthy of one's political support. Interestingly, while conservatives historically have been less confident about the capacities of the populace and its government to attain a just society, they have been quite optimistic about the capacity of a capitalistic economy (also a human construction) to provide a better life for more people if freed from governmental restraints.

Relatively few Christians in our society have moved beyond establishment thinking to become advocates of socialism or to join one of the several, small socialist parties in the United States. Those who do espouse socialism are likely to do so as a theoretical option with little opportunity or inclination to identify with a group that seeks to realize socialist objectives through political action. The appeal of socialism to these Christians often results from first-hand exposure to poverty in our society, compelling the question of whether an economic system that effects a more equal distribution of goods and services is not more worthy of support. These Christians are convinced that an economic system based on the acquisitive, selfish nature of human beings is bound to result in a society that is ruled by these instincts and that accordingly suffers from their excesses.

A more radical stance among Christians is seen today in liberation theology, emerging in Latin America in the 1960s and exerting considerable impact in North America among theologians and certain segments of the church. Its advocates stress a radical discontinuity in their views from those we have thus far discussed. Christians who are either conservative or liberal in their theology or in their political and economic philosophy still represent ideological views that support the establishment. While liberals are more critical of the establishment, they are still fundamentally committed to it. Advocates of liberation theology would make a decisive break with the ecclesiastical, political, and economic establishment, stressing the need to transform it

and committing themselves to fundamental social change. Theologically, this means that the starting point for "doing theology"
is not Scripture and tradition but the life and experience of the
poor, the exploited and marginalized of society. This starting
point transforms theology itself from attempts to think about
reality to a commitment to change it, from concern about orthodoxy to a concern about orthopraxy, or the actual life and
practice of the church as it seeks to be a catalyst for the emergence
of a just society—the liberation of the masses.

This shift from theology as right thinking to theology as
right practice reflects the impact of Karl Marx, who saw the
purpose of philosophy as no longer *interpreting* the world but
transforming it. The influence of Marx is readily acknowledged
by liberation theology, but advocates argue that they are simply
utilizing those aspects of Marx's thought that are helpful in understanding society and the plight of the poor. They find Marx
to be insightful in his analysis of society as a class struggle, but
they separate this social analysis from his materialist, atheistic
philosophy and thus claim to remove the incompatibility between
Marx and Christian faith.[3] Marx becomes the servant of the
Christian community in providing the analytical framework for
understanding social conflict.

Liberation theology embodies such a radical commitment
to social change that it redefines the church's witness in terms
of a prophetic ministry on behalf of the poor. It identifies the
source of the church's power and inspiration with the poor in
their encounter with Jesus Christ, giving rise to a spirituality that
can and will effect profound social change. One must remember
that the political and economic context for the birth of liberation
theology is one of abject poverty for masses of people and a
cynical oppression of the majority by a privileged few. The im-
mense suffering and hopelessness of the peasant population form
an imperative to the church, that it be an agent of social change
and transformation. The criterion for the church's authenticity
becomes its capacity to serve the poor and to enable them to
transform their existence.

Throughout these pages, we have spoken of love and connected love with the quest for justice in society. Liberationists

speak in yet stronger terms in insisting that love remains an abstraction if it does not move us to become involved in the class struggle on behalf of the poor. Love that is authentic takes the form of class solidarity and social struggle.[4] In this struggle, the Christian imperative is often identified with socialism as a means of realizing the common good, in contrast to capitalism with its emphasis on competition. In spite of the dependency on Marx and the espousal of socialism appropriate to the situation in Latin America, advocates of liberation theology maintain that they are falsely accused of ideological bondage. On the contrary, their emphasis upon social change and transformation is one that attacks ideology, whose function (as defined by liberation theologians) is always to preserve and maintain the prevailing order. Liberation theology maintains a critical and polemical relationship with existing society, looking forward to an ideal that is promised by the future rather than realized in the present. This intention, which is essential to the integrity of liberation theology, also poses its particular challenge.

Without question, the economic order in Latin American countries, which locks the vast majority of the population in poverty and hopelessness, needs changing. This predicament is so desperate and overpowering that liberation theology is moved to place Christian faith itself in the service of the revolutionary struggle, identifying the faith with the goals of the new, anticipated order. The struggle for liberation takes on an all-consuming human dimension that would transcend the economic and political measures that are utilized to attain it. Christianity becomes a means toward reaching the exalted goal, but the problem is that the idealistic goal of the movement can never be divorced from the political and economic measures that would realize it. A socialist ideology informs the revolution, which in turn can become the occasion for a new system of bondage. The lesson is clear: The Christian message should never be made the means to attain any particular political or economic order, regardless how noble or idealistic the intentions of the reformers. The challenge for liberationists is to encourage vehicles for change without losing their capacity to keep a critical distance from the new, ensuing order.

Liberationists are also vulnerable to the presumption that Marxism is a "scientific" theory that unmasks prevailing ideologies but transcends ideology itself. This deception should not convince the person of faith. Quite apart from the claim to being scientific, which history would make difficult to prove, Marxism has often betrayed an incapacity to exercise a self-critical spirit that would challenge its claim to possess the truth. Without recognizing a truth that places all of our truths under judgment, we will inevitably absolutize our own version of the truth and justify every means in order to attain it. Such has been the tragic story of Marxist communism.

Even as this point is made, however, the Christian must acknowledge with sorrow that the church itself is fully capable of exercising a similar hubris, claiming to possess the truth and using it as a club with which to rout its opponents. Whenever this happens, the church is peculiarly guilty because its faith should resist this misuse of the truth. Faith in God is at the same time our confession that we do not *possess* the truth; the truth possesses us. The gospel of Jesus Christ is the truth that makes us free; it is always sovereign over our expression of it, and that is why the truth invites our allegiance rather than coercing it. The truth is not reducible to either a finished orthopraxy or orthodoxy, a fact that both Christians on the Left and Christians on the Right can find difficult to recognize.

Christians on the Right

As a religion identified with the political and economic establishment, Christianity in North America (whether lower, middle, or upper class in its ecclesiastical expression) tends to be supportive of conservative values. While one can make distinctions between mainline and fundamentalist-evangelical churches, all of them express at both leadership and grassroot levels a political and economic orientation that is basically accepting of the prevailing order. Politicians in this country have learned long ago that appeals to religion or "religious values" can be highly effective when arguing on behalf of the status quo. Ideological groups that have been most successful in gaining religious support are usually those that have appealed to the conservative instincts of believers.

Our discussion of Christians on the Left led us beyond the usual perimeters of liberalism to liberation theology as a more radical expression of the Left. The same is true when we turn to Christians on the Right, where we encounter a more radical expression of conservative thinking in those Christians who are identified with "the New Religious Right," or what we will call the Religious Right. The impact of Christians in this camp has been far more pronounced in the United States than the impact of those advocating liberation theology, reflecting the conservative character of church and society in this country. Liberation theology is discussed in these pages more as an illustration of a response from the Left, while the Religious Right constitutes a concrete option that appeals to significant numbers throughout many of the mainline churches.

While we often identify the Religious Right with fundamentalists and conservative evangelicals, it is necessary to make a closer identification. Gabriel Fackre notes five groups within the evangelical-fundamentalist spectrum, the first three including many who are associated with the Religious Right.[5]

1. *Fundamentalists* are characterized by a strict biblical inerrancy view and a separatist stance in relation to other Christian groups; they are militant in the defense of their doctrines. While some are apolitical, those who are politically active make up the core of the Religious Right.

2. *Old Evangelicals* stress the "born again" conversion experience and may or may not be politically involved.

3. *New Evangelicals* identify with the magazine *Christianity Today* and are more likely to insist on the relevance of their faith for political and economic life.

4. *Justice and Peace Evangelicals* identify with the magazines *Sojourners* and *The Other Side*; these Christians stress the radical critique that biblical Christianity brings to contemporary culture.

5. *Charismatic Evangelicals* are often apolitical and stress the gifts of the Spirit, such as speaking in tongues and faith healing.

A distinctive dimension of the Religious Right is the role played by television evangelists and the tremendous impact of the media in spreading the ideology of this movement. TV personalities like Jerry Falwell, Jim Robison, and Pat Robertson have contributed powerfully to the success of the Religious Right, exhorting their viewers to become politically involved. The traditional focus of these evangelists and of fundamentalists and evangelicals generally has been the individual who is exhorted to accept the gospel of Jesus Christ. They see the issue as spiritual, not political, transcending the realm of politics and social issues of any kind. However, the Religious Right recognizes to its credit that the gospel speaks to the individual in society and that the faithful life is not lived in a vacuum but in the real world, where political action makes a difference in fashioning society.

What marks the program of the Religious Right, as in every right-wing group, is the restoration of a more simple and secure past. A strong nostalgia is at work that idealizes a previous era, posing an answer from the past to the present threat of a more complex and swiftly changing world. The most threatening change that confronts Religious Right believers is the erosion of belief, or loss of transcendence (the "absence of God"), in a secularized age. It is an accurate reading of our time and one that must be taken seriously, but the answer posed by the Religious Right is essentially dominated by fear over a world that seems to be losing its stability and direction. The response of fear is often to take refuge in a retreat to the past or to blame the powers that be—whether secular humanists, the Soviet Union, or the Democratic Party.

Pluralism, which we noted in chapter 1 is a threat as well as an opportunity to the Christian church, is perceived by the Religious Right as a direct consequence of the loosening grip of the Christian tradition on the public life of our society. Those on the Religious Right see it reflected in the widening gap between state and church, one effect of which is the exclusion of the Christian heritage from the education of our youth. To the Religious Right, people of influence who are imbued by the spirit of secularism appear intent on stripping our religious heritage from national consciousness, and consequently a battle must be fought to maintain religious teachings and practice in the public schools. The lines of battle have been drawn over issues such as praying to begin the school day, the teaching of creationism in biology classes, and the right of religious student groups to meet on school premises.

One can appreciate the concern of these Christians that our religious heritage continue as a strong and vital source of direction to the life of our nation. We have noted the moral crisis that we face, and certainly Christians should be alert to any evidence of the unraveling of the moral fabric of society. What hinders the cogency of the Religious Right response is the fear and insecurity that appears to drive it. When a movement or group is dominated by fear, it poses a threat to those values that are at the heart of a democratic society. It imposes its viewpoints and "solutions" to social issues rather than engaging in dialogue and seeking consensus; it is vulnerable to extremism, for if we are fearful enough, a solution must be found at all costs and as quickly as possible. Insecurity and fear lead to the suppression of free discourse and the exchange of ideas, for only absolutes and simplistic truth can satisfy the fearful warrior. This attitude, of course, not only threatens our civil traditions but contradicts the mind and attitude of faith, which looks to the future with humble confidence in the sovereignty of God. The social arena, important as it is, remains the *penultimate* realm of our lives; the kingdom of God transcends whatever we accomplish or fail to accomplish in this life.

The politics of fear in which the Religious Right is engaged also makes it vulnerable to ideological arguments and causes. Its adherence to the ideological right is pronounced and often extreme, without much if any indication that the church's message should be distinguished from political and economic beliefs. While liberation theology is vulnerable to the appeal of socialist ideology, the Religious Right will unabashedly support capitalism on grounds of Scripture itself. Religious Right adherents commonly establish the rightness of their ideological positions by quoting the Bible, thus baptizing them with the authority of God. This encourages absolutist positions that do not allow for alternative views among either Christians or non-Christians.

Another disturbing feature of the Religious Right is its apparent blindness to many areas of social injustice. The one social issue that has galvanized considerable activity among Religious Right adherents is abortion, which they overwhelmingly oppose with little willingness to acknowledge any exceptions. Other issues such as racism, poverty, and the environment do not generally excite their attention because these are not perceived as conservative issues. Any discussion of war and peace reveals a pronounced patriotism if not chauvinism. The United States is exalted as a chosen nation, favored by God and bearing a divine mission in the world. Here the lack of capacity or willingness to be self-critical is often apparent. One's nation is the ultimate power and source of security to which fearful people can repair, and the more insecure one is the more exalted does the nation become.

Finally, related to the chauvinistic attitudes of the Religious Right is its inclination to demonize the Soviet Union as the enemy of God's people. This is characteristic again of fearful people who want an obvious enemy to bear the blame for the world's problems. Communism as an abstraction is synonymous with the essence of evil or Satan. This belief encourages notions of a "holy war" against communism. Perhaps this is the most sobering feature posed by the Religious Right, given the potential destructiveness of a nuclear war. How ironic indeed if Christians were to be a serious obstacle to the resolution of tensions between the two superpowers; when the enemy is demonized, negotiation and compromise are not options. Thus one hears the presumptuous language of Armageddon, which presumes that we as a nation are chosen by God to usher in the close of human history by vanquishing the enemy. One can understand that the present easing of tensions between the United States and the Soviet Union is not particularly welcome to people with these convictions. We can expect a continuing effort from the Right to dramatize every possible conflict between the Soviet Union and the United States, and to question the reality of an authentic transformation in Soviet politics.

Christians of every denomination must challenge the thinking and attitudes of the Religious Right. We risk giving the impression to the rest of society that the vocal Christians on the Right are expressing the dominant Christian viewpoint. What they are actually doing is prostituting the Christian message by placing it in what they perceive to be the service of their nation. They consequently contribute to the polarizing of the world community and encourage the notion that the enemy is beyond the boundaries of Christian concern. In contrast, a profoundly Christian perspective and hope is expressed by Herbert Butterfield in regard to international conflict: "Even in time of war, when passion can hardly be kept from rising high, all sanity depends on our keeping, deep at the bottom of everything, some remembrance of that humanity which we have in common with our bitterest enemies. It may be a prejudice of mine, but I wonder whether Christians, if they could disentangle their minds from the conventional mundane systems that constitute them, might not within a decade contribute something creative to this deeper cause of human understanding."[6]

Beyond Ideology: The Quest for Community

The common features between Christians on the Left and on the Right are profound disillusionment with things as they are and a vision that promises a transformation of society. Each side is yearning for a utopia—whether in a promised future or an idealized past—and the prospect of realizing it generates the fervor and momentum of their efforts. To achieve the transformation, however, would necessitate complete control of society with sanctions and coercive actions more characteristic of totalitarian governments than of a democratic one. The political realization of one's moral and theological vision poses some particularly tenacious obstacles, the more so when one's vision promises a fundamental reordering of society. While this is a common problem for Christians at both ends of the ideological spectrum, one must acknowledge the significant difference between the vision of the liberationists and that of the Religious Right. The former bring a vision that is dominated by an authentic concern for justice that reaches out to the oppressed. The Religious Right, on the other hand, yearns for a kind of Christian society that betrays the self-interest of middle-class Americans who want to guarantee an order that will secure themselves and their country.

While none of us is unaffected by the ideologies of our time, an authentic Christian responsibility should prevent us from being predictably ideological in our thinking and acting, whether from the Left or the Right. Some, undoubtedly, will regard the contents of this book as much too ideologically slanted on behalf of the poor, and yet one cannot deny the biblical basis for this concern. Its validity and importance are recognized by adherents of both Left and Right; the genuine conflict is in our judgments concerning the seriousness of various social inequalities and in the means by which they are to be addressed. Here I acknowledge a personal bias on behalf of an active role on the part of government. I would hope, however, that this conviction is appropriately balanced by an ingrained suspicion of governmental bureaucracies and the recognition that honest and competent leadership as well as built-in checks and balances are necessary to effective governmental action. On a given issue at a given time, a particular ideological position may represent a reasonably accurate and responsible judgment. However, since every ideological position also reflects the vested interest of a group, one cannot assume that position uncritically. At the same time, one ought not be naive about the pervasive role of self-interest in generating political action. Our system of government encourages the active involvement of groups and individuals who are motivated to accomplish political goals that reflect their interests and concerns, as long as they remain within the limits set by law. But Christian concerns about justice will keep in focus the legitimate interests of those who have no organizational or financial power. Christians must be concerned to give a political voice to those who cannot be heard in spite of the legitimacy of their concerns.

The concern for justice is essential to establishing a society that achieves a significant measure of community. This continuing struggle is never completely realized, but where the concerns of justice are prominent, polarities of class and race are more adequately addressed and a healthier level of integration is achieved. The issue for Christians is not ideological purity but establishing a measure of justice that enables all segments of society to overcome the ravages of poverty and discrimination and to experience a sense of belonging and of participating in the common life of the nation. This will not happen without a strong tradition of good faith and justice in the land, a tradition to which Christians in particular—both individually and corporately—should be actively contributing.

In our country at the present time, the primary temptation facing large segments of the Christian community is to think that our society is basically sound and deserving of commendation for achieving high levels of personal freedom, economic wealth, and opportunities for individual and corporate development. Complacency and self-satisfaction have always been the primary temptation of churches whose members are solidly middle class. We can indeed be thankful for the remarkable democratic heritage of this nation and the part our own religious tradition has played in its development. But we can never afford to lose our sensitivity to ways in which that system is warped and skewed by those in power. We have reason to be thankful for the material blessings that have been showered on this nation, but those blessings must not blind us to the growing disparity between the rich and the poor and the destructive potential which that development holds for the future of all of us.

The church, as well as society at large, needs to be challenged to move beyond a spirit of complacency and to recognize the assaults being made on the moral and social fabric of our nation. The current drug crisis may serve as a costly lesson to alert us to the seriousness of our problems. Drugs are the opium of a society that is sick; we recognize it in the hopelessness and despair of the underclass as well as in the ennui and spiritual emptiness of the middle and upper classes who have lost their religious and moral roots. This crisis can serve us if it occasions a serious evaluation of our moral health as a nation and renews our incentive to get our priorities straight in addressing some of our deep-rooted social problems. The church's tradition and its social conscience can contribute precisely at this point.

The church can also help this nation move beyond the tired ideological conflicts that divide our people and that fuel the international conflicts between East and West. The church transcends national boundaries and is capable of bringing a global vision to our people, but too often it has done little more than provide religious support for our nation's own agenda. The self-critical spirit Christians should bring to the public discussion is not a sign of weakness or evidence of lukewarm commitment to our country or to its democratic traditions. On the contrary, Christians in every nation who are truly informed by their faith will subject the ideals and causes of their country to the enduring values of justice and truth. Christians will raise the radical questions that challenge the establishment in which both liberals and conservatives have a stake. At the same time we are called to participate as responsible citizens in the common life of our people, thankful for the measure of justice and idealism that characterize our life together. We should neither forsake nor exalt the political and economic traditions that sustain us, recognizing that the former is an act of cynicism and despair while the latter is an act of idolatry.

The important thing is that we recognize those goals for our society on which we can agree and acknowledge our common commitments to them regardless of our ideological stance. Defining these goals helps us to see our unity; our differences are more likely to emerge in what we think should be done to realize them. Liberals will rely on greater involvement of the federal government to rectify injustice; their concerns will center on the working class and their right to a fair share of the nation's wealth. Conservatives will exalt the capacities of the private sector to create a just and viable society and the need to attack the economic ills of the worker by priming the productive pump—for example, by providing a friendly tax system for the business community. Reducing the antagonisms that emerge from these two approaches is paramount, and Christian involvement in that task will stress the goals common to both approaches and will challenge the doctrinaire, absolutist expressions of either side.

In addition to ideological polarities, in recent years we have witnessed a proliferation of interest groups that are intent on exerting the political pressure that will enable them to achieve their goals. Whether it is the Gray Panthers or gays and lesbians, unions or trade associations, educators or farmers, groups motivated by what they perceive as issues of justice or by purely economic motives will spend considerable amounts of money to make an impact upon those in positions of power and influence. Christians and their churches should recognize their responsibility to emphasize the larger picture and to help people to be attentive to the common good as well as the good of their group. This means that we should be concerned to gauge the impact of our own group's demands upon the common good. It means that we are committed to dialogue and the recognition that accommodation is necessary if everyone is to share in the fruits of a just society. Unfortunately, the stress on competition and adversarial relations in our society does not serve to develop a strong social ethic that recognizes the interdependence of all groups and segments of our population. The sense that we need each other and that we are all in this together needs to be cultivated more aggressively by the Christian community in the days ahead. An increasing number of our citizens are ready to understand this language.[7]

The task of realizing community grows more difficult with the passing of time. The growing heterogeneity of our people is profound, embracing race, color, class, language, and culture. People who live in adjacent apartments can be living in such different cultural worlds that they can hardly communicate. Their understandings of morality and human destiny are so diverse that one might despair of reaching a common mind on any matter of importance. The gift of Christian faith at this point is the recognition that every creature is precious, created in God's image. We are children of God, sharing the divine image that bestows transcendent value no human agency can remove. Our differences can be celebrated, but more important, our unity as God's children provides a common bond that engenders respect and the desire to understand and appreciate each other. The Christian faith will not let us deny this unity; it binds us together and gives us courage to face our common future.

Let us return one last time to the two couples in chapter 1, John and Blanche and Fred and Tina. In them, we saw the conflict within the church between those who find the church's response to social issues as the primary realm of our Christian witness and those who would avoid social issues and focus on the individual's faithfulness to the gospel message. Often these viewpoints reflect ideological stances rather than a viewpoint that is carefully developed on theological and ethical grounds. For this reason, the conflict between Christians at each of these poles is often intense and a source of embarrassment to the church. If the thesis of this book is correct, however, no exclusiveness exists between our individual and corporate responsibility as Christians. Following Jesus Christ is a matter of both individual and community discipleship. As Christians, we are the church, impelled both as individuals and as the church to exercise our freedom in Christ in ways that testify to God's love and reveal a heightened sense of responsibility to our neighbor.

Our consideration of moral decision making at both individual and corporate levels has stressed a number of things that are important to remember:

1. As individual Christians and as a church, we need to be clear about who we are and the nature of our faith, if we are to know what it means to be faithful.

2. Our confidence as Christians in making moral decisions rests in the conviction that God is merciful; we dare to act boldly because grace abounds.

3. The Christian life involves our response to both law and gospel, God's Word that both orders and constrains our lives and inspires us to selfless action on behalf of our neighbor.

4. Responsible moral decision making involves being informed, whether acting as an individual or as a community of faith.

5. Though we want certainty in the form of absolutes (a biblical directive) and clear answers to what is the morally right thing to do, we can seldom reach that certainty on the more challenging life situations and issues we face.

6. Responsible moral decision making requires the capacity to be self-critical, recognizing our tendency both as individuals and as groups to act in ways that are self-serving.

7. Our Christian responsibility reaches out to the whole of creation and to all people, claiming a unity and interdependence rooted in the one Creator who is Lord of all.

The Christian life in its individual and corporate form is ultimately a matter of being faithful. While that may sound simplistic, it does involve a variety of dimensions, many of which we have discussed in our consideration of moral decision making. The moral life often appears to be terribly complicated and personally distressing, and one hopes for the kind of support and counsel that can and should be available in the Christian community. Moral decision making is a struggle from within as we deal with our own weaknesses and from without as we seek to cope with difficult and complex circumstances that defy our best intentions. But the struggle is worth our best efforts, for it is one in which we are literally defining ourselves as human beings. For the Christian, this self-definition occurs in knowing the freedom bestowed by the gospel, acting in a spirit of love toward one's neighbor, and thereby living responsibly in meeting the demands of life.

Notes

Preface

1. Among recent works on the subject are David Cook, *The Moral Maze* (London: SPCK, 1986); James Gaffney, *Matters of Faith and Morals* (Kansas City: Sheed and Ward, 1987); Richard Higginson, *Dilemmas: A Christian Approach to Moral Decision Making* (Louisville: Westminster John Knox, 1989); Lewis B. Smedes, *Choices: Making Right Decisions in a Complex World* (New York: Harper & Row, 1986); and Louis B. Weeks, *Making Ethical Decisions* (Philadelphia: Westminster, 1987).

1: Being a Christian in Today's World

1. *The Washington Post*, national weekly edition, 22–28 February 1988.
2. Elton Trueblood, *The Predicament of Modern Man* (New York: Harper & Brothers, 1951).
3. *The Christian Science Monitor*, 7 October 1986.
4. Howard G. Garner, "Children of the 'Society on the Take,' " in Paul T. Jersild and Dale A. Johnson, eds., *Moral Issues and Christian Response*, 3d ed. (New York: Holt, Rinehart and Winston, 1983), 11.
5. Quoted in *The Washington Spectator* 13, no. 11 (June 1, 1987): 1.
6. Robert N. Bellah et al., *Habits of the Heart: Individualism and Commitment in American Life* (New York: Harper & Row, 1985). "Habits of the heart" is the expression of the nineteenth-century Frenchman, Alexis de Tocqueville, in describing the mores or elements of character that mark a society.
7. Ibid., 6.
8. Ibid., 77.
9. Ibid., 130.

2: The Bible as Authority for Moral Life

1. To speak of the Bible as a "resource" for the moral life could lead to misunderstanding. It does not mean that the Bible is simply a passive object

123

to which one turns to pick out the relevant passages. The Christian does not "use" the Bible in this sense but is actively engaged by its message and enters into dialogue with it. There is reverence before the authority of Scripture that is rooted in Jesus Christ, but at the same time one must approach the written word in a spirit of critical study in order to understand its message and interpret it responsibly as it relates to the moral life.

2. There are many helpful works on the subject of the Bible and the moral life of the Christian, including the following: Bruce Birch and Larry Rasmussen, *The Bible and Ethics in the Christian Life*, rev. ed. (Minneapolis: Augsburg, 1988); James Gustafson, *Theology and Christian Ethics* (Philadelphia: United Church Press, 1974), chap. 6; J. L. Houlden, *Ethics and the New Testament* (New York: Oxford University Press, 1977); R. N. Longenecker, *New Testament Social Ethics for Today* (Grand Rapids: Eerdmans, 1984); and Thomas W. Ogletree, *The Use of the Bible in Christian Ethics* (Philadelphia: Fortress, 1983).

3. A Greek word for love, *agape*, is commonly used in our language to express the distinctive meaning of love within the Christian context. It is love as defined by the gospel of Jesus Christ, the offering up of oneself on behalf of another. This agapeic love expresses the meaning of love as we discuss it here, which is not to deny the importance of other expressions of love for others— as in friendship and erotic love.

4. See Paul Ramsey, *Basic Christian Ethics* (Chicago: University of Chicago Press, 1980), 24ff.

3: From Convictions to Decisions

1. People who "do ethics" usually make a distinction between *ethics* and *morality*, denoting the former as reflection about moral behavior and the latter as the behavior itself. Usage in this book usually follows that distinction. At the same time, popular usage will often dictate the appropriate expression to use. "Moral decision making," as in our title, could more consistently be labeled "ethical decision making" because making decisions is a process of reflection about moral behavior and would normally precede or lead to certain kinds of behavior. We use the term *moral* instead because of common usage that gives it a more comfortable sound.

2. Among Christian ethicists who represent this emphasis, most prominent is Stanley Hauerwas. See his *Truthfulness and Tragedy* (Notre Dame, Ind. : Univ. of Notre Dame Press, 1977), *Vision and Virtue* (Notre Dame, Ind.: Fides, 1974), and *A Community of Character* (Notre Dame, Ind.: Univ. of Notre Dame Press, 1983). Recent works of Alasdair MacIntyre have been particularly influential for Hauerwas and others in developing a "virtue" ethics. See MacIntyre's *After Virtue: A Study in Moral Theory*, 2d ed. (Notre Dame, Ind.: Univ. of Notre Dame Press, 1984).

3. Hauerwas, *Truthfulness and Tragedy*, 20.

4. Ibid., 26ff.

5. The novice cannot easily get a handle on the writings of Søren Kierkegaard, whose works are a fascinating mixture of autobiography and profound reflection on the human journey. The best book to begin with is his own explanation of his works, *The Point of View for My Work as an Author*, trans. Walter Lowrie (London: Oxford University Press, 1939).

6. The most readily recognized, if not the most balanced, advocate of situation ethics has been Joseph Fletcher. See his *Situation Ethics* (Philadelphia: Westminster, 1966) and *Moral Responsibility* (Philadelphia: Westminster, 1967). Another term often used to express a similar point is *contextual ethics*, as in the work of Paul Lehmann (*Ethics in a Christian Context* [New York: Harper & Row, 1963]).

7. Fletcher, *Situation Ethics*, 31ff.

8. The fact that this incident occurs under the conditions of warfare is a complication that might lead us to justify many acts that would be unacceptable under peaceful conditions. Nonetheless, nations have attempted to retain some degree of humaneness in the midst of the inhumanity of war by adopting agreements that would protect prisoners from wanton violence and torture on the part of their captors.

9. H. Richard Niebuhr, *The Responsible Self* (New York: Harper & Row, 1963), 89.

10. Ibid., 75.

4: Facing Some Moral Dilemmas

1. This point is made by Martin Luther in his understanding of Christian freedom: "Christian freedom is not bound to any particular work, for all works which come along are of equal worth to a Christian. The shepherds did not run off to the desert, don cowls, shave their heads, or change any of their external practices in clothing, time, food, or drink. They returned instead to serve God by caring for their flocks." Quoted in William Lazareth, ed., *The Left Hand of God* (Philadelphia: Fortress Press, 1976), 144.

2. A critical question here is the impact of an industry on the moral health of the nation, a question that in some cases could conceivably be argued both ways. Should one regard employment on the staff of a magazine producing a comparatively mild form of erotica or employment in the liquor industry as appropriate expressions of one's Christian vocation? What about employment in a company manufacturing military hardware? Is there a decisive moral distinction between involvement in producing conventional weapons in contrast to producing nuclear weapons?

The problem inherent to these questions is that one can cite potential values as well as potential harm in each of these products. One can defend or lament the need being met. Even nuclear warheads can be argued as necessary to deterring their use on the part of a potential enemy. It is understandable that the more ambiguous the moral decision becomes, the more likely we are to leave it to the moral discernment of the individual.

3. *The World Almanac and Book of Facts, 1987* (New York: Pharos Books, 1986), 769.

4. For the sake of simplifying references to male and female homosexual people (gays and lesbians), we will often use *gay* as a comprehensive term referring to all homosexual people.

5. Our discussion of this subject here is necessarily much too brief. The reader is referred to a helpful volume that provides an overview of the assessments currently being made by Christian theologians concerning homosexuality, from

negative to positive viewpoints: Edward Batchelor Jr., ed., *Homosexuality and Ethics* (New York: Pilgrim Press, 1980).

6. Robin Scroggs, *The New Testament and Homosexuality* (Philadelphia: Fortress Press, 1983).

5: The Church in Society

1. The implications of this idea are spelled out particularly well by Lesslie Newbigin, *Foolishness to the Greeks: The Gospel and Western Culture* (Grand Rapids: Eerdmans, 1986).

2. Many more distinctions can be made, of course, in describing the mission and witness of the church, but this basic twofold character of its witness should be reflected in all that the church does.

3. Larry Rasmussen, "Going Public: The Church's Roles," in Charles P. Lutz, ed., *God, Goods, and the Common Good* (Minneapolis: Augsburg, 1987), 29–43.

4. Robert F. Blomquist, "Getting the Lay of the Land: The Congregation's Task in Social Ministry," *Lutheran Forum* vol. 12, n. 2 (Pentecost 1978):10–12.

6: Christians on the Left and Right

1. This necessary openness to understanding the concerns of opposing sides reminds one of the astute observation made by John Stuart Mill: "He who knows only his own side of the case knows little of that" (*On Liberty* [New York: Liberal Arts Press, 1956], 21).

2. Herbert Butterfield, *International Conflict in the Twentieth Century: A Christian View* (New York: Harper & Brothers, 1960). The American theologian and social ethicist Reinhold Niebuhr provides a similar insight in his classic work *Moral Man and Immoral Society* (New York: Scribners, 1932).

3. José Miguez-Bonino, *Doing Theology in a Revolutionary Situation* (Philadelphia: Fortress Press, 1975), 98.

4. Peter Hebblethwaite, *The Christian-Marxist Dialogue and Beyond* (London: Dartman, Longman & Todd, 1977), 53.

5. See Gabriel Fackre, *The Religious Right and Christian Faith* (Grand Rapids: Eerdmans, 1982), 6–7.

6. Herbert Butterfield, *International Conflict*, 28.

7. This problem includes something as close to home as our taxes and the failure of our society to effectively tax the affluent so that a meaningful support system is maintained for people struggling with poverty. This does not happen in a society like ours without a strong social conscience on the part of the whole society, and particularly on the part of those in power. Our capacity to reach out in voluntary acts of mercy and compassion is often heartwarming, but as a society we have often failed in our humanitarian obligations to those unable to help themselves. Conservatives and liberals will disagree on how best to address this issue with the tools of government, but we have no excuse for a failure of will to take those measures that will most effectively address and counteract poverty and the human devastation it creates.

Index

CPSIA information can be obtained at www.ICGtesting.com
Printed in the USA
LVOW102146150812

294454LV00001B/39/P